Advance Praise

"Sherri Coale is one of my favorite storytellers. She has such an incredible way of piecing together the perfect words to move you emotionally. You'll probably cry multiple times while reading her stories. The Compost File will inspire you to be a better friend, spouse, mom/dad, leader, and quite frankly, a better overall person. Buy it. Read it. Implement what you've learned. And then buy one for all your friends. They'll thank you later."

— **Ryan Hawk,** Host of *The Learning Leader Show,* Author of *Welcome to Management, The Pursuit of Excellence,* and *The Score That Matters*

"Coach Coale touches the reader's heart with moving stories drawn from real life and she offers practical, scripture-based examples of how we can each rise to the occasion becoming better neighbors, better citizens, and better people. This is a must read."

— **Mo Anderson,** Former CEO and Board Member of Keller Williams Realty International

"Coach has poetically done it again. Forced us to look beneath the surface of our daily lives, at the seemingly simple victories and the heroes and lessons at the heart of them. She paints stories that we can all relate to, perhaps that we take for granted. It's a perfect reminder to stay present, in gratitude and appreciation, for the signs

i

and gifts that are revealing themselves around us. The Compost File is a win for all of us."

— **Stacey Dales**, Senior National Reporter - NFL Network

"Sherri Coale has crafted a heartfelt and deeply inspiring collection that resonates with anyone striving to make their mark. 'The Compost File' captures the grit, resilience, and humanity that fuel personal and professional success. A must-read for anyone navigating life's challenges with determination and heart."

— **Jason Blum**, Blumhouse CEO & Founder

"Sherri Coale has quickly become one of my favorite writers. The definition of a Coach is to make people better. Sherri will make you better by reading her book. She started by teasing me with her blogs and then she sat me down with her first book, Rooted to Rise. She has a gift of storytelling that keeps you wanting more. She sees more than most and shares experiences, strength and hope through clarity of word while painting a picture you can touch and feel. I can't wait to share this book with others."

— **Clint Hurdle**, 17-year MLB Manager and author of *Hurdle-isms: Wit & Wisdom from a Lifetime in Baseball*

"We all need coaches. Athletes need help finding their hidden best, and all athletes should read this as a guide to elite performance in competition. But the rest of us also need motivation, inspiration, intensity, focus and faith. All that lives inside these covers."

— **Wright Thompson**, author of *The Cost of These Dreams*

"Legendary basketball coach Sherri Coale has combined simplicity with movie-like vision in this hugely inspiring book that applies wisdom to winning off the court. Rich with meditations on everything from the benefits of composting to the selfless dedication of school crossing guards, this collection offers a beautiful new way to think about the everyday."

— **Hannah Karp**, Editorial Director, *Billboard*

If you know Sherri, I'm sure you have already realized this, she can entertain anyone with her God-gifted storytelling. But what makes her words so valuable is she observes what others miss. Hence, her wonderfully crafted stories reveal the importance of things we fail to notice. Her words open our minds to understanding and appreciating the wonders found in life's in-between moments, those forgotten seconds, that thanks to this book, I am reminded to remember and embrace once more.

I may know wiser people, but if I do, none of them are able to break down life experiences and life lessons into the context of life applications as well as Sherri Coale. And that's the reason I hated when I'd turned the last page. I wanted more! That's the power of well written prose.

— **Ace Collins**, Best-Selling Author

Full of wit, wisdom and years of experience coaching. There is something for everyone to enjoy and learn.

— **Mark Victor Hansen**, 59-times #1 *New York Times* Bestselling Author

STORIES FOR THE
STRIVER IN US ALL

The Compost File

By

Sherri Coale

Photo Credits - Green couch pic - Chandler Coale, Chandler Rae Photography
Head shot - Shevaun Williams, Shevaun Williams and Associates
Creative contribution - J.C. Plaza
Book Layout - DBree

Manufactured and printed in the United States of America
distributed globally by markvictorhansenlibrary.com
New York | Los Angeles | London | Sydney

ISBN: 979-8-88581-179-8 Hardback

ISBN: 979-8-88581-178-1 Paperback

ISBN: 979-8-88581-180-4 eBook

Library of Congress Control Number: 2024923912

For those addicted to "yet"

For years, I've kept a folder on my laptop. In it go things I think . . .
things I love . . . things I do not understand.
I named the portfolio "The Compost File" because what's in it
helps me grow.

Benefits of Composting

Enriches soil, helping retain moisture and
suppress plant diseases and pests.

Reduces the need for chemical fertilizers.

Encourages the production of beneficial bacteria and fungi
that break down organic matter to create humus,
a rich nutrient-filled material.

Table of Contents

Introduction

Some people are born with an ear for music, or an eye for painting. Others are gifted communicators, or incredible mentors and teachers. But it's the truly generous person who chooses to share their talent with others. Sherri Coale is one of those people. Her storytelling, wisdom and lived experience help the rest of us make sense of life; inspiring and offering strength, spotlighting the moments where God is at work, in butterflies, a child's art project, or the memory of a loving parent. It's as if Sherri were born with X-ray vision for how to see and process life's wonderful, joyful, heartbreaking and confusing moments, while turning them into useful nuggets.

The act of writing is not for sissies. Getting what you want to say out of your heart, into your head and onto the page is often frustrating. But the essays in this book take everyday experiences, encounters and thoughts and spin them into something magic, with deeper meaning and connection to family, friends, faith and a good dose of funny.

I met Sherri in Oklahoma City, walking toward me with a giant smile, gorgeous blonde hair and rocking a pair of four-inch stilettos as if they were Air Jordans. I liked this woman instantly, and we've stayed in touch ever since. When I read her first book, our friendship was sealed. And each time her blog lands in my in-box, I find myself nodding and smiling as I read. When she asked me to write this introduction, I was honored.

Many know Sherri Coale as a star player at Oklahoma Christian University, garnering more wins and awards than I can tally, and she'd hate it if I did. As the winningest coach in the University of Oklahoma women's basketball history, she built a powerhouse program in Norman, with teams appearing in 19 straight NCAA tournaments and three Final Fours. Sherri is a member of the Women's Basketball Hall of Fame, the Oklahoma Sports Hall of Fame, the Oklahoma Women's Hall of Fame, the Oklahoma Christian Hall of Fame, the Norman High School Wall of Fame, and has "Home of" signs that flank the entrances to her hometown of Healdton, where her tight knit, humble upbringing formed the backbone of her can-do attitude, tireless work ethic and desire to lead with kindness and generosity.

And that takes us back to Sherri the person, the master motivator, devoted friend and daughter, engaging speaker, wife to Dane for 37 years, mother to two children and adoring grandmother to two beautiful little girls who are a frequent subject of her musings. Deep down, Sherri is still the girl from a small town in Oklahoma, thirty miles to the right side of the Red River, who fell in love with reading, writing and basketball, though not necessarily in that order. She connects her past to our own, the early years playing basketball, going to IHOP or the 7-Eleven, her memories of grandparents, getting called home for dinner, the feeling of unconditional love and wide, open skies.

One of the most poignant essays in this book is about running, lacing up her sneakers to pound out the miles, as a way of dealing with the fear and sorrow during her mother's bout with a serious illness. "Hard things are funny like that," she writes. "They take all your money, punch you in the gut, leave you for ruin, and then hand you a voucher with no expiration date and call you a cab."

I love Sherri's take on the middle place in life, that amorphous spot between young and old, wherever it lies. "We just look up one day and realize that we're there," in a place where "the tough and the tremendous are in cahoots together." Just when it can feel like the clock is running out, Sherri reminds us we can change the scoreboard, as she cheers us from the sidelines.

Despite the trophies and life's shiny accolades, she urges us to give randomness a chance. She shows us what resilience looks like, and how to get back up when we've had the wind knocked out of us, reminding us that "the 'just abouts' are just about as good as it ever gets."

In the end, the common thread is Sherri's clear and beautiful storytelling voice. This is a collection of life's lessons learned at home, on the basketball court, through traveling the world and living life fully. They are the stories of everyday grace, of compassion and connection, of contributions of spirit and soul. I know you will enjoy each one of these pearls which collectively form the resplendent necklace of the book you are about to read.

— Lee Woodruff
New York Times bestselling author of *In An Instant*

1

Just About

The front man of Vampire Weekend was once asked how the band's fifth album could measure up to the success of their Grammy-winning fourth. He said that his philosophy of production was more a revelation of a whole than the stacking of a thing that's somehow superior to the thing that came before.

He explained, "It's like if you're showing someone around the United States, and you started out in Los Angeles—if the person has never seen the rest of America, they might say, 'OK, I get it. America is filled with palm trees, sunshine, the film industry, and celebrities.' And then you'd go, 'No, no, that's just L.A. Wait until I show you North Dakota.'"

What a rush to know the end's not dead. Something else is out there waiting to be known.

Maybe

I love a road that's just about to bend. A season that's just about to start. A concept that's just about to gel enough to actually become a thing. Energy lives in those 'just about' moments. The giddy kind that makes you think there is no lid on the sky.

Always and *Nevers* are skinny slivers with not much room for play. But *almosts* have lots of space where imagination can run and jump. The possibility that lies right around the corner from an *almost* beckons like a giant index finger curling itself back toward its palm. You might get what you think you want. You might get something better. You might not get anything but more of the same. You might get a bottomless pit. There is no way to be sure about what's coming. Not really. Even if you've been down that road a thousand times before.

That's what gives 'just abouts' their punch. Possibility floats around, above, and in between them like red and yellow leaves on a windy autumn day.

When my daughter was in preschool, she came home one day with a crooked stick about ten inches long and as big around as her daddy's thumb. It was gray and gnarly like the ones we use for kindling when we start a fire. But this particular stick was wrapped in all kinds of colorful paraphernalia. Bright pink ribbon, orange pipe cleaners and a fancy cobalt-blue fuzzy tie with a marble on the end adorned it like Sunday finery. The stick looked like a magnificent art project, but I could tell it carried more weight than that. I was most curious to find out why.

"This is cool!" I said. "What is it?"

To which my precocious four-year-old replied, "It's a possibilities stick."

I could not have been more intrigued.

"A possibilities stick," I said aloud, trying to get my brain to catch up with the words.

"Yeah," she said, "This is what you hold when you want to make something possible."

"Like a magic wand?" I asked.

"No. It's for real stuff," she said, with her four-year-old serious eyes.

Could there ever, in the history of ever, be a more interesting creative project at school?

Overwhelmed by the visionary thinking of a teacher steeped in Play-Doh and finger paint, I could hardly wait to ask my daughter's Pre-K instructor about it at parent-teacher night. When I did, we shared a pretty good laugh.

She told me what the students made in class were talking sticks. You held them when it was your turn to speak. That's how the almost-ready-for-school kids learned to communicate in a group. But that's not what my Chandler heard. Oh, the way some things land differently on individual ears and hearts! The teacher and I both agreed that while it might be tough in application, 'possibilities' was a much better name for the stick wearing colorful clothes.

I have no idea where my daughter's interpretation came from, but we used it every chance we got through the years, and the colorful stick still sits on a shelf in my house. Sometimes I randomly pick it up when the road is about to curve.

This cusp of newness, the place where possibility lives, is a space we don't have a name for yet. 'Just about' is the fulcrum on which some die a thousand deaths, but it's also the place where it's hard for most of us to control our happy feet. Ask any athlete about how it feels the night before the season's opening game. Of all the games that happen after, nothing ever feels the same. When the concert is just about to start, when the bride is just about to walk down the aisle, when the baby is just about to emerge from the canal and show you her giant sky-blue eyes, life feels bouncy. Anticipation is not a big enough word for that.

"'Well,' said Pooh, 'what I like best,' and then he had to stop and think. Because although Eating Honey was a very good thing to do, there was a moment just before you began to eat it, which was better than when you were, but he didn't know what it was called."
— A. A. Milne (1928)

I hear you, Pooh. I feel it right before the tulips bloom, and the cold front hits, and the chorus strikes in a "God Who Listens." My heart gets the zoomies like toddlers get right before it's time for bed.

Years ago—before upside down squeeze bottles—Heinz Ketchup had an ad campaign anchored by Carly Simon's chart-topping hit, "Anticipation." Each commercial's arc takes us from fast-paced to slow-mo living. As a burger sits suspended, ornery children pause. Babysitters lean to look. Chins fall into hands. Frenzy halts as all eagerly anticipate the emergence of the thick red condiment from the bottle. The tag line read: "Worth the Wait."

Some things are. And some things aren't. But the right-before part rarely disappoints.

The 'just abouts' are just about as good as it ever gets.

A Million Ways

Go write. And please don't try to get it right. Just write. Because trying to do it the way you think it's supposed to be done only gets in the way.

The daily practice of writing is a foundational habit loads of successful people share. Daily writing grounds busy minds. It serves as a conveyor belt for sorting thoughts, ideas, philosophies, relationships and emotions. It leads people out of corners they have backed or worked their way into by revealing doors and windows they weren't aware were there. And yet just as many folks who do write don't—because they think they don't know how.

How is not the point. There are a million ways.

Unfortunately, we live in a *right-way-wrong-way* world. Especially in business where lots of zeros follow dollar signs and organizational charts rule the day. We want to know, for sure, how to get from here to there. Discover-as-you-go feels like unnecessary gambling. We are way more comfortable with an outline to follow where sequential steps lead to more sequential steps that lead to other levels until prowess is attained. A linear pathway is the road of preference to get to the Promised Land. We get anxious if the stepping-stones are not laid out for us to see.

But straight lines don't account for differences in people or the jagged nature of terrain.

"The way is made by walking," the poet Antonio Machado famously said. So much of what makes us good at anything worth being good at is what we can only learn as we go. And what we do with what we discover depends on our unique DNA. The footprints of success leave clues we'd be wise to stay attentive to, but we must walk in our own way.

That means embracing uncertainty. Leaning into curiosity. Placing awareness at the top of our list of things to do. Context is ever-changing, as are we and those around us, so fool-proof plans are typically anything but. Recipes just don't exist for all things.

There's not a secret combination that opens the vault. Pursuits like writing, drawing, and building—leading, parenting, and loving—don't come with color-by-number guides. Good ideas abound, but there is no formula for getting it *right*. The process is messy. It just is. And though squinting and groping sometimes are haphazard, they make up part of the way.

I used to tell my players, "Beautiful offense arrives from continuous decision making." Decisions based on a context constantly in flux. Defense was rule-based. But offense—at least the freeing kind of motion we liked to play—was principle-based. And while core concepts served as anchors, what a player at any and every moment decided to do depended on all kinds of things—where she was on the floor . . . where the ball was . . . where her defender was . . . where the other defenders were . . . where her teammates were. These all factored into what she did and when she did it. What made a possession work hinged on a bevy of unpredictable things she had to sense at the time.

That meant the *how* was not a blueprint you could memorize or rinse and repeat.

And it made some of our players crazy.

For those who needed to be *right,* it felt like a torture chamber void of any snatch-able absolutes. Questions without clear-cut answers made them nervous. They craved to "know the way." And yet the ones most afraid of the dark would be the first to tell you the best basketball we ever played was the result of figuring out the moments as they came.

At a country music awards show, Blake Shelton performed Toby Keith's blockbuster single, "Who's Your Daddy?" as part of a tribute honoring the legend who was receiving the first-ever People's Choice Icon Award. Shelton's rendition was spot on. True to form and fashion. Exquisitely done. I can't imagine how he—or anyone else, for that matter—could have done it any better. But it wasn't Toby Keith. That bourbon-smooth vibrato only comes from one set of cords.

That's what makes a star a star. A leader a leader, a writer a writer, a mom a mom, and a dad a dad. What can't be written down on paper and copied to a *T* is what makes a thing work in the end. *We* are the variable. *We* are the part that can't be taught but must be constantly rediscovered. *We* are the connector of the proverbial dots. Dots which can be strung together in at least a million ways.

Giving Chance a Chance

Before my freshman year of high school, I wrote on a small piece of notebook paper,

    1. Go to State.

    2. Be an All-Stater.

    3. Get a full ride.

Then I ripped the paper from its spiral wiring and taped it—curly edges and all—to the inside back of my royal blue locker. Those three things were what I wanted more than anything. So, every day during my freshman year when I would go to my locker to gather my books and supplies for first hour, I'd read:

    1. Go to State.

    2. Be an All-Stater.

3. Get a Full Ride.

When the bell rang at the close of class, I'd return to my locker and read:

1. Go to State.
2. Be an All-Stater.
3. Get a Full Ride.

Six times a day for the one-hundred-eighty days of our school year, my eyes told my brain and my body what to do.

When pick-your-locker day arrived for sophomore year, I transferred the *to-do list* to its new metal home in an adjacent hall. There, six times a day for nine more months, my decisions were governed by the homemade billboard:

1. Go to State.
2. Be an All-Stater.
3. Get a Full Ride.

That dilapidated piece of paper traveled on with me to my junior hallway and then to its final destination senior year. It became the GPS for how I spent my high school days. For four years, when my friends went to the Dairy Queen for lunch, I stayed in the gym where I could consume a peanut butter and jelly sandwich while making two-hundred free throws before afternoon classes resumed. Saturday mornings were reserved for workouts, as was Sunday after church, evenings after track practice, and gaps in between homework and rehearsing for the school play. My days and nights were scheduled end-to-end.

I had things to do.

In the summer of 1983, my teammates and I bounced out the back of the gymnasium to board a big yellow bus with blue and white streamers taped to the mirrors, chalky-white shoe polish on the windows, and Lady Bulldog goodie bags in every seat. The bus pulled around to the front of the school where the entire student body perched waiting on the lawn. The band was playing the fight song as our classmates clapped in rhythm while cheerleaders pulsed enormous pompoms in the air. At the stop sign, we took a left toward Main Street, where business owners and members of the community armed with cowbells and good-luck signs lined the street. "GO DOGS!" bounced back and forth in the rearview mirror escorting us out of town.

Anybody who would have wanted to could have stolen Healdton, Oklahoma that day because "closed" signs were in the store windows and the streets had neither people nor cars. Everybody within shouting distance had gone to the State Tournament in Oklahoma City to watch their girls play ball.

Two weeks later, I got up at five in the morning with no alarm clock needed for rousing, pulled a coat on over my pajamas, slipped into a pair of tennis shoes and drove to Mom's Minit Mart to buy a Daily Oklahoman newspaper. It was Sunday, the day the high school girls' All-State team would be announced. Biting the inside of my bottom lip, I carefully unfolded the sections on the living room floor, pulling the cold, crisp pages apart until I found "SPORTS."

And there it was. Small West Squad. My name. My picture. Two down, one to go.

Three weeks later, I signed a letter of intent to attend Oklahoma Christian College on a full basketball scholarship.

A spring of validation for years of dreaming big.

I don't know why I decided to write down my goals, much less put them in a place where I could read them every day. But that raggedy piece of paper in the back of my locker became my rudder. It pushed me toward where I wanted to go while steering me away from where I didn't. So much of accomplishing anything is remembering what you want.

Looking back, though, I'm amazed at all I never considered.

It never crossed my mind that so much of my being able to reach my goals would be outside of my control. I never thought about potential injuries—my own or my teammates'. I never thought about how indiscriminate plays—both our opponents' and ours—influence the outcome of games. How one made free throw here or one missed lay-up there could have sent our season in an entirely different direction than it went. And I never considered how an entirely different direction would not only have impacted goal number one, but also the probability of numbers two and three. Without our team's success, I never would have been named to the All-State squad. And without being named to the All-State squad, I probably would never have received a college scholarship. One had to happen so the other had a chance, and randomness was everywhere.

I think I thought I was in charge of it all. Ludicrous. I know.

That fringy piece of paper taped to the back of my locker was not responsible for what came to fruition. But neither was it a coincidental aside. Without it, there's no way what happened happens. The faded, tattered scrawl carried no promises, nor did it have the power to change the winds of fate, but what it did was birth a process that put me in the ready position to snag what was up for grabs.

Day after day of remembering what you want gives chance a chance to matter. That, in and of itself, is fantastic news. But the even greater news is that the side benefits far outlive whatever we might get for our toil.

I wish I'd held on to that janky piece of paper. If I had, I'd put it in a frame. Not as a badge representing what I chased down and was fortunate enough to catch, but more as a reminder of the breezy winds of happenstance that sometimes do and sometimes don't get in the way.

2
Periphery

Context matters. We aren't shaped in a vacuum. We are molded, at least in part, by who and what bumps up against us.

Our surroundings, whether meticulously selected or thrust upon us by the universe, influence the complexion of our lives.

Sometimes the edges bend and twist with us, sometimes they confine us, sometimes they relax and let us through. But one way or another, our surroundings influence who we become.

Real Life Clubs

I've never been big on clubs. The picking, parceling and politicking. The initiations and the rules. And yet, I've long been somewhat in awe of the way barriers come down when a Kappa meets a Kappa in an airport Starbucks line. Organizations of inclusion—and exclusion, per definition—crisscross the striations of our society. Some have formal boxes to be checked, complete with dues and requirements and the sharing of secret handshakes, pins, and codes. But just as many co-exist organically, without any expectation of bending to become. They form from shared experience—the roads we walk together even though we're far apart.

I've been in a lot of those real-life, no-by-law clubs through the years. The student-athlete club was the one I first realized in real time. As collegiate athletes (regardless of sport), we were connected by weekends and summers that looked eerily the same and vastly unlike our other friends' who were not on a team. Spring break and Christmas vacation meant quick hellos and goodbyes and days and days of ghostlike dorms. Our college experience was a different one than those who didn't play. We were balancing, striving, aspiring. In so doing, we shared an unspoken understanding of both the glitter and the grind. The club was a place where we could laugh and cry without seeming ungrateful, weak, or entitled. We had a language those who got to go on ski trips couldn't understand.

Once my playing days ended and I embarked on a career in education, I became a member of the teachers' club. I was a formal member of both state and national educational organizations for sure, but more importantly, I became a member of the tribe of professionals who stood daily in front of a room full of kids knowing that we didn't know nearly as much our students assumed we did. Naked terror brought us together even if we never made the fear form words inside our mouths. Parking lot duty and painful faculty meetings gave us invisible sticking points while attendance sheets and grading scales kept us tethered in mundanity as we fought the ever-growing bureaucracy threatening to stand between us and the doing of our jobs. We bonded over knowing how much our work mattered while also knowing that no matter how hard we stretched to reach, we'd never be able to touch all the hands. Such intimate understanding makes fast friends. When a teacher meets a teacher, the walls come tumbling down.

Not long after I became a member of the teachers' club, I joined the working moms' club. Then the taxi-cab parent club. Then the empty-nester club. One association handed the baton to the next as the membership of each did their best to help one another dodge the bullets and make the curves. None of us had any answers, though we all had composite knowledge of what the questions were. We just sort of quietly trudged along separately together. Through glances, waves and been-there-done-that shoulder hugs, we kept each other afloat. It's strange the solace you can find in simply knowing someone else is also bleeding out.

Nothing binds quite like shared experience. That's why teammates remain teammates long after jerseys have been retired. It's also why strangers sometimes walk through gates of natural human safekeeping—because they, too, have sat in the chair or stood by the bed or pulled off to the shoulder of the road to cry. The moments that have no words unite them. Real-life clubs have dues their members pay by living. That's how you get in. The kind of community found inside sustains us.

Most recently, I've become a member of the coveted Grandbaby Club. It's the only club that's named for what you get instead of what you do, though what you do are all the things you never thought you would. It's like Disneyland in here. It doesn't matter where you are, what you're doing, or who you think you're talking to. If you say, "I have a grandbaby," to somebody in the club, the member does a back flip and you join her at the hip. It's as if a giant easement appears connecting the best parts of both of you to each other, and you each become a person you recognize but aren't entirely sure you know. A lighter, sillier version of the original. You connect in a space that has no name in a cloud of giddy joy.

Organic affiliations are like that. The companionships don't always make sense, but differences don't much matter because similarities are so strong. We make our way by walking through the same stuff, at the same time, and the walking is made better by the company we keep.

Gives and Takes

During the Covid lockdown of 2020, I got a dog. Well, technically, I didn't. Our family did. We got a dog. Or more specifically, our adult daughter, who had returned home as a pandemic boarder, did. She got a dog who lived in *our* home. Rosco, who sort of belongs to all of us, was Chandler's dream—long, long deferred.

For as far back as I can remember, Chan had wanted a dog. As a young girl, she loved picture books of puppies, then movies about dogs. In high school, she had a collection of puppy faces and frolicking fur-ball videos on her smartphone. She would show them to me from time to time to test the waters. "Looooook!" she would swoon while shoving the phone in my face.

"Awwww," I would boomerang back, simultaneously enamored with the image and completely aware that what she was asking for was not just a dog but a dog who could live in her room with her. And sleep on our couch. And beg at our feet when we sat down to eat. And bark . . . and pee on the carpet . . . and shed.

Over and over, every time she asked, "Mom, can I pleeeeeease?" my answer was invariably the same, though I half-heartedly tried to act as if I gave it consideration.

"Not in the house. Not in *my* house, ever."

Oh, the famous last words of parents! "Ever" came much sooner than I'd planned.

I grew up having dogs as pets. Fawn and Coco—two mutts from the same litter who looked absolutely nothing alike—were like siblings to my brother and me. Siblings, that is, who lived outside. In a doghouse. On the patio. In *weather*. (Gasp! Shock! Abhorrence!) I was raised to believe this is how it works. Cows, horses, sheep, foxes, cats, *and* dogs—creatures who walk on four legs instead of two—live outdoors. They're built for the elements. They need room to run and roam. Humans, on the other hand, live indoors. We need kitchens and bathrooms, television screens and couches. People live in. Pets live out. Everybody has a place.

Enter Rosco, the spunky French Brittany Spaniel who stretched all my boundary lines.

Chandler and her dad organized the puppy acquisition behind my back while I was busy doing other things (mostly Zooming). Then one day they just matter-of-factly announced they were going to pick up "her dog." Four hours later they walked in the house, Dane carrying sacks of puppy paraphernalia and Chandler cradling Rosco in the crook of her right arm.

Our house hasn't been the same since. I find chew toys in the hallway, shoes in rooms where I didn't leave them, hair on couches, chairs, rugs, and most of the clothes I thought were clean. Chandler and Rosco moved out as the world opened back up, but the anti-doggie-seal on our house broke open for good. Rosco visits regularly and stays with us when Chandler has places to be. His food and water bowl have a permanent spot on the brick paver floor inside our double back doors. We keep a basket of his toys beside the couch. Leashes, brushes, and treats have a reserved spot on a shelf behind the bar. And he's not the only four-legged friend who now pretends he owns the place. Our son, Colton, and his wife, Morgan, have a Golden Retriever and a French Brittany of their own (named respectively Sohie and Ace) who also come and go as *they* please.

Our house is a grand hotel for dogs.

I wish I could say I'm a fan of this arrangement, but I can't. Because I'm not. The panting, the drooling, the vet bills, the shedding, the occasional five-alarm bark. They're every bit as annoying as I once imagined they would be. Yet, somehow, all I knew I'd hate is overshadowed by all I never dreamed there would be to love.

It's the Cracker Jack surprise of give and take.

I wouldn't trade a hairless house for the enthusiastic arrival, the get-as-close-to-you-as-I-possibly-can when nobody else is home, the perking of the ears with a head tilt when I pose a question. These pups are practically human, but they don't judge or know how to hold a grudge. They simply come spreading joy, and their legs for a belly rub, along with a side of slobber. They wear you down with happy, no matter how much armor you have on.

And that's just what I get from the dogs. The multiplied blessings come from the mixture of them with us, them with them, and us with us. The love that careens off one living thing and slams into another creates a matrix of connections that fortifies our air.

Scarcely, if ever, do we love the whole of anything or anyone, if I'm being painfully honest. And rarely does a hard line do the tricks that a stretchy one can. Things of merit typically need to suck in here and breathe out there to work right. Marriage. Teamwork. Raising kids. Staying on budget. It's deciding what you want and then deciding again, more acutely, what you want even more. A concession here. A give-back there. A deep sigh of toleration with a look the other way can unearth wonder. Sometimes what we don't like can lead to what we love.

I loved teaching in the public-school classroom. I detested grading papers. I love planting flowers. I do not enjoy spraying for insects and disease. I love going shopping. I hate trying things on. Whether we like it or not, most *gets* come attached to fairly substantial *gives.*

Family dinners at our house these days are a fiasco. When a cat passes by outside the window, the world turns upside down. I vacuum sometimes thrice a day.

But Rosco warms my feet when I'm typing. And sometimes during dinner, I pet Sophie under the table with my toes.

The *gives* have clearly lapped the *takes.*

Ever Ready

I'm a classic pre-liver. Whenever something big is coming, I take it for a test drive before it actually arrives. I do the hills, the sharp turns, the narrow parking spaces that appear to be too skinny for a fit. Just me and *the big deal.* A time or two or twenty, we hit the road to go for a spin, so she won't feel so foreign in real time.

Pre-living, for the record, is not the same as doomsday prepping. Neither is it exactly like dress rehearsing. Or trouble borrowing. Or some sort of aversion therapy, though the conditioning piece applies.

Pre-living is *what if* reckoning. A way of getting some reps before the amorphous, daunting unknown.

When my kids were young, the first day of school was a hairy monster scratching on windows and lurking at the edge of the driveway. The frightful morning I'd have to dress my offspring, feed them, and hand them over to the world was a mini-movie that cued itself, randomly running when I'd take off on a jog or jump in the shower or be putting laundry away. I lived it over and over before I had to. I suppose to make sure I could.

As the kids grew older, I rode with all kinds of upcoming rites of passage in the twilight before they were real. Proms, play-off games, college applications . . . then the biggie—graduation. I built up my endurance like a runner training for the Boston Marathon or the Running of the Bulls at Pamplona, Spain.. My heart put in the time. Then, when the moment finally happened— whatever shape it arrived in—I knew we could get along.

Big deals aren't always attached to the hip of my children, though when the kids were small, it seemed like almost every deal was big. Sometimes the terrifying stranger is an impending re-location, an event, a new job, or a diagnosis.

A few months after retirement, at a doctor's appointment to address an old injury (the kind that simply refuses to go quietly away) I didn't get the verdict I wanted. The news, however, didn't faze me. What I mentally danced with in the thirty minutes between the x-rays and the doctor talking, made his diagnosis feel almost like a gift. My foray into the future built a bed I could tumble into. It smelled of sweet relief.

What pre-livers create in the futuristic land of make-believe are opportunities for both pleasant surprises and disappointing letdowns. The bad that we envision has great odds of being not so bad, but the good can sometimes have a hard time living up. This

Russian roulette does not, however, deter us. As John Milton said, "The mind is its own place." So, we exercise our right to traipse through our respective versions of Heaven *and* Hell - we like to cover all our bases. Like the Boy Scouts, those of us who wade in possibility love to live prepared.

Pre-living is purposeful because it helps us do what's hard before we have to do it. At least that's what I tell myself when I'm trying to turn the habit into an admirable character trait. It helps me consider options, play out scenarios, try on different hats for size.

It makes me feel like I'm doing due diligence. *I can do it if it happens this way. I can do it if it happens that way.* It's like a parlor game. Mostly fun. Sometimes enlightening. Occasionally kind of scary. Something for my brain and heart to engage in while I'm waiting to figure out what I'm supposed to do with my hands and my feet.

I used to envy, a bit, the mother who didn't shed a tear as she ushered her children across thresholds. The one who was happy to drop off her mini-me at kindergarten, eager to be on her way. She, who also whooped and hollered at high school graduation and couldn't wait to turn the adolescent cave down the hall into a workout room, is an anomaly to me. A superhero of sorts wearing an invisible cape, but clearly not a pre-liver. She's a cross-the-bridge-when-you-get-to-it girl. A proud card-carrying member of the "What Happens Happens" club. She and I go through the world in different ways.

The Pre-Liver Cult, of which I am a disciple, prefers to be there *before* we get there. We can be found building parts for the superhero's bridge on the opposite side of the street.

Pre-living is sweaty, roll-your-sleeves-up kind of work, even though it's effort screwed into a cloud. But we members of the cult don't mind. We wrestle and toil not to predict or sear an expectation, but to be ready when whatever's bound to be finally is.

3
Uphill Climbs

The long slow grind of uphill scaling is scary, exhausting, and hardly ever comes with a hint of a how-to map.

If you asked my knees, they'd tell you the hardest part of going up is coming down.

But up and down come linked—a package deal that tests both nerve and patience. Hills expose us, dare us, and taunt us with their real and imaginary limit lines.

A crucible changes us. We're different after the climb.

The Impossibles

The 6'3" center on my college basketball team drove a lovingly used black Volkswagen Beetle. Watching her unfurl from its tight confines was entertaining, but it paled compared to the ride. Most of our teammates and I drove cars varying in size, form and functionality. But hers was the one we took when we were more about the *going* than the *where*. The Bug was perfect for short jaunts from the gym to the dorm when the undeterred north wind was howling and we, soaked with sweat, needed to get from point A to point B (preferably without catching pneumonia). It was our vehicle of choice for a 7-Eleven Slurpee or a stack of pancakes at IHOP. It was what we took when we had nowhere to be but felt the urge to go. As the point guard—aka, the only one who could fit—my spot was in the backseat behind the driver, knees tucked under chin.

On our compact liberal arts campus, the roads went around, not through. These circuitous paths that hugged our "city on a hill" weren't flanked on the exterior by curbs or landscaped hedges or parallel-parking spots. Only grass stretched out beyond them as a moat. We used to joke that the design was either meant to detain us or to form a boundary to keep the riffraff out. Mostly, the encircling roads made it impossible to get anywhere in a hurry. Overzealous campus cops made sure of that.

Oddly, in one frequently passed spot, on a grassy expanse to the south of the dorms, two metal poles jutted up from the ground with a patch of concrete between them. It looked as if someone had once envisioned a walking bridge to span the culvert but got sidetracked along the way. From the road, the opening seemed maybe wide enough for a couple of people to walk through shoulder-to-shoulder. The kind of thing you notice without ever thinking about.

Until the day you do.

Late on a nondescript fall afternoon, while waiting for the cafeteria to open, a couple of my teammates and I decided to go for a drive. Still belting the REO Speedwagon hit that was bellowing through our hallway, we piled into the Bug with the kind of freedom that lands on you when you're not where you were, but you're not yet entrenched in where you are going to be.

I had scarcely *assumed my position* when out of nowhere I heard our driver—my relied upon center, the one whose sure hands and soft touch earned me around six assists per game—say, "Hey guys, you think we can fit?"

"Fit? Fit what? Where?"

"Through here!" she shouted as she released the clutch and gunned it. Before I could even wrap my head around what was happening, the Bug was flying toward the makeshift gate in the middle of the grassy field like a missile aimed at the moon.

I closed my eyes and screamed.

Within seconds that ticked like forever, we were bouncing across the field through and beyond the metal posts that we'd just split on a diagonal path toward a parking lot that led to the four-lane street. Dizzy with adrenalin and in a stupor spawned by shock, we slowed to a stop and let the rush sink in. I could not make it make sense. Never in a million years would I have dreamed a car—even a tiny one like a Bug—would fit between those poles. I couldn't imagine there was a fingernail's space left over on either side. Incredulous, I looked out the back window at the teensy-weensy opening we had somehow cruised right through.

As the revelation washed over us, we shrieked in unison before doubling over with laughter, each of us holding our ribs and flailing until we couldn't breathe. The piercing of the illusion continued to juice us for days.

Then we did it again. And again.

And then we stuffed different teammates in the car and did it yet again. Before long, it was a gauntlet we passed through while in mid-sentence (though the rush never completely went away) to short-cut our way to the street. From seemingly out of nowhere, the once-incomprehensible threshold became the path we took. Our eyes don't always tell us what we need to know.

It didn't take too long for the campus cops to catch on to our game and put a lid on the frequency with which we could use our now not-so-secret route. Sometimes as I'd drive past the "gate," I'd glance at the metal posts and nostalgically marvel at our teammate's chutzpah while arguing with myself about whether the car could actually fit. Though our eyes don't intend to deceive us, they can make impossible real.

"You can't get there from here," I often think and sometimes say, whether I'm trying to make it to the interstate through a maze of rural back roads or attempting to reach consensus on a subject with paralyzed sides. An impasse can look so daunting from an outside perch. When what my eyes see and what my brain tells me are two completely different things, I'm reminded of the way that wasn't—until we chose to take it. Risky faith in action. Part of doing what doesn't seem doable is trusting yourself to give it a shot.

Run, Forrest, Run!

I *hate* running. But I *love* having run. In the small town where I grew up, in high school, everybody did everything. We had to. There weren't enough people to go around. So, football players marched in their shoulder pads with the band at halftime, and basketball players ran track in the spring after the state tournament was over (whether we wanted to or not). My senior year, our school hired a new basketball coach who instituted cross country, so I learned to do that, too. That's just the way it worked in a single-stoplight town.

To get to what you wanted to do, you had to do some stuff that you didn't. That's one of those lessons that doesn't get you much mileage on the ACT but has a pretty good payoff in life.

In high school track, each member of the team could be involved in up to four events at meets. I ran the lead-off leg on three sprint relays and my individual event was the open quarter mile. I loved the relays (even if I wasn't particularly fond of the running). I loved the significance of the hand-off—how much it mattered, how much it had to be practiced, how much trust and concentration were involved. I also loved that our anchor leg was so good that if we got her the baton anywhere close to the other racers, we'd usually win the race. I'd fly out of the starting blocks, run my leg, hand off the baton, then high-tail it (regardless the distance of the leg) back across the middle of the track to the finish line, the spot from which I had only seconds earlier taken off, to greet our last leg as she crossed the tape. I loved being connected like that. Our relay teams were tight four-person families who ran separately together tracking time toward a prize.

But I'd like to punch the open quarter in the face. The quarter mile is a gut-check race. You run it by yourself, without the luxury of an anchor to catch you up when you fall behind. It's one lap around the track, basically in a full sprint—or as much of one as you can muster—and it never ever gets easier no matter how much you train. It hurt to run it every single time. I hated toeing up at the starting line in my lane assignment. I hated the dreadful first curve. I hated the lonely backside straight-away. I hated the final curve where I started to lose feeling in my legs. I hated the way my glutes cramped the moment I stopped running. I didn't love anything about it. Ever.

Except that once my body recovered, I was convinced there wasn't much I couldn't do.

That's the thing about hard things.

Thirteen years ago, on the day of my mom's first biopsy, we ran our own sort of open quarter. The space between the test and the verdict was a slog. We knew it was cancer, but we didn't know how bad, so we spent the day dancing with demons. It was the classic "I-don't-know-if-I-can-do-this-but-I'm-not-sure-I-have-a-choice" swirling in my mind every time I lined up on the track for my individual quarter mile, waiting for the starter to raise and fire his gun. The significance of one juxtaposed against the insignificance of the other is not lost on me. However, the sinew required to get through both is, eerily, basically the same.

Mom's ultimate diagnosis, treatment, and recovery had plenty of uphill stretches. We ran long distances—her, obviously, far more than me. But the hardest part, for me, was the day of waiting. We walked and talked and hung out on the patio in my backyard, staring at the phone—willing it to ring. I remember the dread, the lonely, the numb . . . and the cramping of relief that came in a rush at the end. But once the day was over, we were emboldened. Whatever would be required of us next was something we knew we could do.

Hard things are funny like that. They take all your money, punch you in the gut, leave you for ruin, and then hand you a voucher with no expiration date and call you a cab. The tussle changes the landscape. I think that's why I still like *having* run.

I ran the open quarter for my track team because my track coach, who was also my basketball coach, told me to. Track was the plus-one riding shotgun alongside basketball, so I did what I needed to do. As it turned out, the quarter mile was a great race for me (a little speed, a lot of stubborn). My running it helped our team pile up points where our unlikely band of runners won and won and won. We were even crowned State Champs in 1982. They gave us medals, trophies and a blue and gold letterman's jacket with a state of Oklahoma patch on the front. Though I can't say I loved running, I've always been glad I did.

The stuff we got for winning is in a plastic tub somewhere, I'm sure. But those weren't the spoils I took with me from my days spent circling a red cinder track. For starters, running taught me about discipline. My friend who's a former professional runner, says, "It's the one sport you can't hide in. If you don't do the work, the world will know." She's right. You do it naked and alone, and your preparation doesn't lie. Running also taught me about focus— the things you are pressured to keep in the forefront of your vision, the places you cannot allow your mind to go. But mostly, I think, running taught me that sometimes you have to do stuff you don't particularly enjoy. And that doing your best, regardless, is the prize.

I go for a run more or less every day, still, and I never want to do it as I walk out my back door. But every single time I finish, I breathe a breath of boldness. Hard things are everywhere. We choose some and some choose us. Either way, the opportunities to be and to be better pile up around our feet. And though it never feels like it at the time, gifts are often waiting on the backside of hard things.

The Chameleon Called Time

Five minutes, when you're waiting for a verdict, a diagnosis, or laying head-toward-floor in a dentist's chair with your mouth propped open on blocks, feels eternal. Seconds drip as if distended, each one clinging mercilessly to the one that came before. But five minutes, when you're reading a powerful page-turner, or playing a game you love, or holding a sweet sleeping baby in your arms, fly. The seconds chase each other in a full-out sprint, barely touching as they hand off the baton.

Rarely do five minutes ever feel the same.

Time is a chameleon, sometimes flowing, sometimes dragging and mostly moving at a speed we do not prefer at the time. We chase it and we curse it as it stretches and shrinks intermittently, ushering us on like an inchworm. We are captives of its pace.

When my kids were young and I would go on a recruiting trip for more than two days, the time between departure and return loomed like a bloated whale. In my head, three days was a lifetime. I would convince myself before leaving that when I got back, the three-year-old I'd left behind would have hair all the way down her back, braces on her teeth, and a prom dress on layaway with matching ankle-strap stiletto heels. Hyperbole is a young mother's superpower. Every drive to the airport reeked of angst. And the minutes while I was gone? They slow-dripped like a leaky bathtub faucet while I watched other people's kids play ball. If a tournament ended early, I'd do almost anything within my power to get home sooner than I'd planned. Red-eye flights and 4 a.m. wake-up calls were the norm. "I'll sleep when they're grown," I told myself. Time puffed up like a dragon and scorched my peace of mind.

For parents and their kids, and eventually kids and their parents, time is a wild horse that cannot be tamed. The days are sometimes tedious inside the minutes, but they gallop on despite our fiercest efforts to rein them in. Our kids leave for kindergarten in the morning and come home at the end of the day with a high school diploma in their hands. Where does the middle go? One day our dads are fixing the roof and the next we're hiding the car keys from them and picking up a walker at the local Medical Mart.

It's a hurry-up-wait-a-minute cadence. The way Father Time usually travels when carrying people and things that we love.

Time may march in uniformity, but that's rarely how we experience it. And though it's neutral, it often shifts in shade depending on our internal perceptions. Like one of those rugs that appears to be mostly blue when looked at with the lay of the pile from one side of the room and mostly tan when looked at against the grain from the other, circumstances color how the clock moves. Time and space shared by two different people can feel massively disparate. A movie flies by for you and drags on for me. Practice, to one player, seems like it just started and to another as if it will never end. The pace time takes is personal.

In downtown Oklahoma City, where the Alfred P. Murrah Federal Building used to be, a memorial now stands. It is flanked on the east and west sides by two giant gates of time. One gate is stamped 9:01 and the other 9:03. The minute that is missing is the one that changed everything.

Sometimes time soars. Sometimes it hovers. And sometimes it appears to stop.

When we look at it over our shoulder, it's difficult to fathom where it has gone. Time is elusive like that. Hard to pin down, hard to accurately measure, and even harder to know what to do with because we never can be sure of how much we have.

4
Attention, Please!

Toward the latter half of the first act of Arthur Miller's "Death of a Salesman," Linda Loman, wife of Willy, the disillusioned, tormented main character, admonishes their grown sons to not look away from their father. She slams her fist on the table and demands, "Attention must be paid!"

It's so easy not to notice.

Chunks of Time

I covet the certainty of young eyes that see so clearly before the world gets in the way.

Austyn, my granddaughter, is almost two-and-a-half and mostly she's clear about what she wants. But what she always knows *for sure* is what she doesn't.

Occasionally, we get to have a sleepover, this angel child and me. She comes to GG's to spend the night, I do a touchdown dance, then we do whatever she wants to do until it's time for her to go home. In between the spoiling, however, I try to get the rituals right. She must finish lunch before she can have a popsicle. We count to ten as she brushes her teeth. And we do our best to save her screen time for where mom and dad try to keep it—right before going to bed. Her favorite videos are held as dessert to help her "wind down" from the day. After her bath and the unchoreographed escapade of putting on her PJs, she runs around the couch like she's at NASCAR looking for the checkered flag. She can't wait to name her pleasure. I go down the list, "Ms. Rachel . . . Cocomelon . . . Blippi . . . Bluey . . .?"

"SLIME VIDEOS!" she screams. It's the unexplainable favorite pastime of children everywhere.

Austyn is glued to my phone, enthralled with the incredulous crunching of slime, when suddenly she comes unwound. "Not this ONE! Not THIS ONE" she chants desperately, her voice rising in octave, tone, and decibel. A bright shade of red is climbing up her face and her eyes look frantic. "NOT THIS ONE!"

"Whoa. Don't panic," I say. "Just tell me what you want. Do not panic," I repeat as I reach to take the phone in search of a preferred episode that will do the winding down.

She responds through staccato, sobby breath. "The rainbow one."

I find it, press the triangle pointing to the right in the center of the screen, and she is immediately happy in every corner of her face.

Fast forward twenty minutes.

Slime time ends. We brush her teeth. Read a book. Say our prayers. "God, please help GG."

I tell her the story of the three bears. Then the three bears mish-mashed with Cinderella. Then the three bears and Cinderella with a Dumbo sighting in the middle. She wants another story still, and I am out of leads. I tell her for the fifteenth time, "It's time to go to sleep." But she keeps talking. I tell her, "It's time. To put. Your Voice. Away." She turns the volume down but keeps conversing with everything in sight. She talks to her stuffed animals, the pictures on the wall, her hands, my elbow . . . for close to an hour she flips and flops and whisper-talks, doing everything within her power not to go to sleep.

I finally come undone.

"Austyn, you HAVE to go to sleep!" my tone shifting from "GG cool" to "Mom-I-Mean-It." She recognizes it immediately and locks her eyes with mine.

"GG, don't panic," she soberly says. And a sly grin slowly spreads across her face as if to say, I know things you have forgotten. Or maybe never really knew.

* * *

A friend of mine went twelve rounds with a tumor in his brain. The war started with a cancer diagnosis that gave him less than six months to live. However, to the surprise of no one who knew him, he bucked the odds and made it over a year. What followed was a tedious, high-risk surgery predicting less than a 50-50 chance of survival. He bet the house and came out smiling on the other side. For the next three years, he was good. Really good. As good as a man can be, that is, with a time bomb in his head. Then one day at a regular check-up, the kind that cancer patients set their emotional watches by, they told him the tumor was "on the aggressive again" and they were out of weapons to try to make it slow its pace.

But you couldn't sniff panic within a mile of this guy.

My friend lived gratefully. Peacefully even, and yet quite far from idle. He was rarely in a rush, but neither did he dawdle. He walked chin-up, eyes-focused-forward, living all the minutes of his days. Like Austyn who has zero tolerance for wasting her precious twenty minutes on a show she's already seen or doesn't love, my friend wanted every single second to count. He didn't engage in drivel, or consume food he didn't like, or feel compelled to keep reading to the end of a not-so-great book. He looked at time as a gift to be unwrapped second by second—even though his chunk had an end he could clearly see.

I first met him, my friend Todd, on The Hill—the nickname for our college campus that to me just referenced the wind. It blew right through us there regardless of where we stood. He was a "city boy" who wore preppy polo shirts, often with the collar turned up, and dock shoes without socks as soon as the weather turned warm. He was a terrific athlete, though he didn't come to school to play a sport, and probably if his grandchild were to ask him, he'd tell her he had no idea what it was he had come to college to do. Or be.

He sure figured it out, though. What a life he lived.

In his final weeks and months—if you went looking— you'd have found him walking in his weighted vest or driving his favorite convertible or with his Bible opened to scripture worshipping God.

His once-searching eyes of translucent blue turned certain. Like the two-year-old who teaches me, he knew some things for sure.

This is the Stuff

I don't do instructions. They give me the heebie-jeebies. The dissecting, the symbols, and the do-not-skip-this steps can make anything feel like quantum physics. I'd rather just mess up a bunch and find my way through. But last Saturday, I waded through a do-it- yourself black- and-white booklet that came crammed inside the first of two giant boxes full of varying sizes of wood along with bags and bags of bolts and screws. In most matters of construction, I go for a run—as far away from the instruction book as humanly possible— and let my husband do the dirty work. Not Saturday, though. Saturday, I was all sixty-nine pages in because we had a swing set to build.

The natural wood playset was our gift to our granddaughter on her second birthday. It was delivered to her parents' driveway on a wooden pallet in heavy, oversized boxes secured by packing straps. They tell you, clearly, when you purchase, that assembly is required. But doubling the price to have a pro come out and put it all together seemed so silly. We are a family with lots of tools.

So, on Saturday we built.

Dane brought a sack of extra devices—like a hundred different drill bits, some random ratchets, and a T-square that turned out to be essential in the early stages of the build. (Who knew? Certainly not me.) I brought a sack of food for grilling, my reading glasses (Thank

God!), our daughter's dog, and a giant box of teddy grahams for the two-year-old birthday girl. Our kids' favorite friends brought elbow grease, optimism, *their* two-year-old daughter, another hammer, and some limes. All totaled, in the fenced-in backyard we had six adults, three dogs, two toddlers, a giant pile of wood with different five-digit numbers stamped on the ends, seventeen sacks of hardware labeled in code, a couple of yellow swing seats, a green double slide, and one sixty-nine-page instruction book.

How could this not be anything but loads and loads of fun?

My daughter-in-law rolled up her sleeves and started sorting, the boys each picked up a tool, and I began barking orders about FW2s and TNT1s while madly rotating the drawings to ascertain if the beveled edge of the board was to be pointed down or up. We deciphered, hammered, drilled, un-drilled, and then re-drilled all over again. We argued and laughed and traded positions when our eyes or our patience or our backs gave out.

Then six-and-a-half short hours later (with only a small pile of left-over hardware we never found a way to use) our girl had a swing set that looked just like the picture beside the button where I'd clicked "buy."

This is the stuff.

Not the swing set, but the building of it—the disorganized, frustrating, funny, unpredictable day with Morgan Wallen singing "Chasing You" in the background and us in shorts and T-shirts getting sunburned in awkward places while blindly decoding a how-to picture book. Six-and-a-half hours on a perfectly good, never-get-again Saturday. Time we can't get back and wouldn't want to because it couldn't have been better spent.

This is the stuff.

Jerry Seinfeld called these "garbage" moments, and he preferred them over quality time:

"I'm a believer in the ordinary and the mundane . . . I don't want quality time. I want the garbage time. That's what I like. You just see them in their room reading a comic book and you get to kind of watch that for a minute, or (having) a bowl of Cheerios at 11 o'clock at night when they're not even supposed to be up. The garbage, that's what I love."

When my kids were small, our family's summers were often spent on the road recruiting, as that was the lifeblood of my job as a Division One head basketball coach. Travel to find players rarely went as planned.

We once found ourselves in Las Vegas, late in the day, with a canceled flight, a hotel room we had already checked out of, and a looming deadline at home the next day. So, we rented a car and made the sixteen-hour trek back to Oklahoma through the night. The kids were around ages six and three, so we stopped a lot. At every detour for snacks or bathroom breaks or gas, we bought a trinket or toy to entertain them the next mile of the way. The back seat of the car grew throughout the cross-country jaunt into an ocean of juice boxes, snack wrappers, sticker books, stuffed animals, French fries, plastic gas station toys, and things that were no longer identifiable because of what they had been through somewhere in west Texas when WWIII broke out.

When we finally pulled into our driveway the following morning, the kids looked like dirty urchins floating in a sea of debris. Chandler's sweaty head was resting on Colton's shoulder and both were finally fast asleep. I quickly snapped a photo because I didn't want to forget. Little did I know at the time, there's no way I ever could. The photo lives, still, in a frame on the edge of my desk.

We've been to Australia and to Rome and up all 1,665 steps to the top of the Eiffel Tower, but the road trip back from Vegas edges out them all. Likewise, the construction-of-the-swing-set day will make the top-ten list.

"Garbage." The kind I live to keep.

Fragile Firsts

Austyn sat up in bed organizing her lovies who were joining us for the night. Turtle-Turtle, Rocky Bear, Dumbo, Puff-Puff and her newest acquisitions from an extended-family gift exchange—Katty and Dog. They were neatly lined up on and around the pillows forming a retaining wall on the far side of the bed. "You hafta be good," she whispered to them. "Santa is seeing who's nice and naughty and he's coming in his sleighhhhhhh!" the last word taking off like a team of reindeer from the roof, its one syllable stretched to capacity inside of her whisper-shriek. I was laying with my back to her, feigning sleep while cataloging every single word as the Times Square Ticker in my head ran 'round and 'round exclaiming, "This is as good as it gets!"

Then she snuggled up behind me, cupped her hands around my ear and whispered, "GG, Santa is bringing you a huge rainbow present. You've been so good." I rolled over, trying to make my eyebrows escalate to the top of my forehead like hers, then we hugged and kicked our feet in unison as the covers flew off the bed. All my pea-sized brain could think was, "Please don't let this end."

I was as happy as any mortal can be. And yet, I was sort of sparring with sad.

I squeezed my eyes and tried to put it in a place where the feel of it couldn't leak out. I wanted to remember how she smelled. How her eyes danced. How her hair looked curling out from under the Santa cap she'd worn to bed. I wanted to remember her voice and her tiny teeth. The way her mind would not stop racing over, under, around, and through this idea of a chubby guy in a red suit with a huge white beard carrying a sack full of toys. She was swimming in the anticipatory thrill of the season—busy elves, flying reindeer, Jingle Bells, snowmen (if only on TV and in blow-up form in neighbors' yards), sugar cookies with purple icing, and CHRISTMAS LIGHTS! I wanted to remember it all.

This is the wonder year. The one and only Christmas Austyn will ever be two. Santa (the good Lord willing) will come back—and he'll keep coming—and she will believe for years. But it won't ever be like *this* again. For the first time, Christmas was a thing. Santa was a man, and flying reindeer and elves who live on shelves somehow made perfect sense. The magic poured down on her like hurricane rain and she romped in the make-believe puddles, as all she couldn't absorb pooled around her feet. With my golden ticket, I watched wistfully, glad to be granted the privilege of a ride on her "AHA!"

Eureka moments are the moments that come with no constraints.

Early in my collegiate basketball coaching career, I asked a peer who'd been there many times, "What's the best part of going to the Final Four?"

"The second you realize you get to go," he said. It sounded ridiculous. But he wasn't wrong.

There were eleven minutes and some change left to play against Colorado when I looked up at the neon scoreboard suspended above half court in Boise, Idaho, and knew. It was an *it-doesn't-get-better-than-this* moment. Our horses were running and the Buffaloes couldn't catch us. I knew we were going to the Final Four.

Tons of amazing stuff followed. Hugs, hats, nets, trophies, police escorts, record crowds. But nothing that happened after ever eclipsed the instant I figured it out. And almost as soon as I grasped it, I felt it slipping away.

That's part of the juju, I suppose. Firsts burn so hot you can't hold them in your hands.

We carry buckets of memories of our firsts around with us in time capsules. The first time we drove a car solo. The first time we served an ace. The first time we got into a fight. The first time we flew in a plane. The first time we saw the ocean. The first time we made love. They live in mental drawers where they don't turn sepia, nor do they grow stale. From there, they tease us with their *firstness*. They have cornered rarified air.

Hence my happy-sad. The stubborn, glorious innocence is unrepeatable. As clearly as I see it, I know it changes shape.

I tried with every strand of my sinew to put Austyn's awe in a bag. I hoarded every facial expression. Every gasp. Every one-finger touch of the ornaments on the tree. Every, "GG LOOK! It's Santa!" Her uninhibited awareness was far too big to keep to herself. Enthusiastically, I accepted every invitation into her wonderland.

As she ripped into her first package on Christmas morning, Austyn exclaimed, "LOOK guys, LOOK!"

Her mom volleyed back, "Whoa! What IS it?"

To which Austyn replied without missing a beat, her bewilderment still at a ten out of ten. "I don't know, but LOOK!"

I yearn for her abandon. The kind that gets hard to reach under layers of living years. But my gloves are tightly laced and I am fighting to be in the moment while fighting to not let it go. Unfortunately, the egg doesn't easily separate from its yolk.

Maybe the two are supposed to live together—the awe and the ache. Maybe because we can't make it last is what makes it so precious as it's happening. Maybe bliss and torment are more like twins than distant cousins. There's so much I don't know.

But one thing I do know for sure—rarely does anything ever compare to the fundamental, fantastic, fragility of firsts.

5

Serve and Return

The Bible tells us, "To whom much has been given, much shall be required."

We stub our toe on *much*. We convince ourselves that required giving means big things—large sums of money, a career serving a third world country, our free time to a cause. And it might.

But that's a swing and a miss at the greater point. We are expected to be helpful. To show up. To be of use.

Taking Care of Those Not Your Own

A lady met me at the door, welcoming me, the guest speaker, to the group's monthly meeting. After a quick exchange of pleasantries, she must have noticed my eyes pass by and then return to the table near the door. On it were piles of greenish-yellow neon vests, signs on sticks, and skinny, orange wands. She answered swiftly and specifically before I even asked.

"We're school crossing guard people," she said, as if reading a sticky label, then peeling back the paper and smacking it to their chests.

Of course, they were—are. Theirs is a century-old organization which commits itself to the kinds of things that make the world a better place while simultaneously keeping our growing city of over 100,000 feeling like a town. The categorical alignment caught me, though. "School crossing guard people." I loved the way these four distinct words sounded in the air, all matter of fact.

A good bit of the room was filled with walkers of their own respective back-nines. Long timers who had been-there-and-done-that, yet wouldn't be anywhere else on the third Thursday of the month at 7:00 a.m. But just as many in attendance were in the throes of deadlines and projects and days that do not end at 5:00 p.m. despite when they begin. A quick glance would not reveal a through-line. The room was a mixed bag of age and gender who stood in unison to salute the flag, pray the prayer, sing the songs, and recite the Four-Way Test. It was peppered with disparate people who together had formed a tribe.

They are school crossing guard people. A subset of a subset that reveals both what they do and who they are.

These are people who show up. And own it. Whatever it might be.

As I made my way past the serve-yourself pot of hot coffee and a box full of breakfast burritos rolled up in foil, I could feel the sturdiness of the room. Not the walls or the roof of the building, but the foundation and character of the people who had simply decided to take on ownership of guiding little people from home to school and back again. I admired their gusto and their pragmatic affiliation. Such sureness isn't all that common anymore. Rarely do people display such sexy pride in doing unsexy things. I knew a lot about them without knowing much at all.

These were people who had clearly moved from the doing of a thing to the importance of getting it done.

There's a hefty difference between those who sign up to serve at crosswalks and those who consider themselves "school crossing guard people." I wondered that morning, in the midst of the ritual of "happy dollars" and paper tablecloths, about the Jello-y space that separates the two.

The civic meeting adjourned as punctually as it began, formal and yet somehow neither stuffy nor absurd. Ironically, crossing guard responsibilities had not been on the agenda. The only mention came as a by-the-way cry that coincided with the "BAM" of the gavel. "Don't forget—school's about to start!" came the prompt, intermingled with the scooting of metal chairs. Evidently, this group didn't need a reminder. I noticed when making my way to the door that the table earlier covered by crossing guard paraphernalia was wiped completely clean. The tennis-ball-colored get-ups were all taken by those who had committed to serve.

These people know who they are. They do not need persuading and they neither balk nor drag.

School crossing guard people are not an ordinary lot. They're more than volunteers who agree to sign up for a time slot. They're heroes dressed in neon who draw hard lines and hold hands softly while wearing humility and courage in layers to be revealed as needed, depending on the day. They are business men and women, retired veterans, grandparents and new parents, singles and widowers, and couples who sign up together to shore up both sides of the street. They are people who assume risks and accept responsibilities. They don't need to be told to be early and they don't have to be asked to stay late.

They are those who made a commitment to take care of those who are not their own.

That's not just a job you sign up for. It's a way you choose to live.

I drove away that morning with Luke Combs' version of "Fast Car" on the radio and this special breed of servants on my mind. "School crossing guard people" embrace the dual existence. They know, at once, that they are inconsequential and invaluable. These are the kind of people who can see themselves simultaneously as a speck of dust in the world and a necessary contributing cog—one safe crossing at a time.

Let The Ripple Run

My dad once ran for school board in the rural village where I grew up. There was some fuss about our superintendent, though specific fuss about what I'm no longer sure (if indeed I ever was). People were wound up. Almost everyone in the fourteen square miles of our oilfield community had pledged allegiance to an opinion and thus had chosen a side. Our tiny town was as fractured as an oil-and-gas pay zone after the drilling was done.

And my dad—of all people—was vying for a chance to enter the fray.

It was beyond out of character for him. Dad hated to be in the middle of anything. Shy by nature, he much preferred to lean against a wall. Though he had staunch political opinions, he was a man who mostly kept his druthers to himself. The spotlight made him break out in hives, so I couldn't imagine what on planet earth had goaded Joe Buben into throwing his hat into this very public ring.

But he did. And he wasn't the one who won.

I don't remember much about the campaign, except that my brother and I were charged with canvassing the neighborhood to knock on doors and hand out flyers (spending most of our time praying no one would be home). The rest is mush. Once the race was over, our life went right back to the way it had been, as if the school board election had never even happened. And the great divide in our splintered town somehow bridged itself.

But I have for decades wondered what got into my dad.

I can only assume he did it because he felt strongly about whatever the fuss was all about. But his courageous attempt at difference-making sent a deeper message to me, and every time an election rolls around, I think about what he did.

I'm not sure my dad ever *really* wanted to serve on the school board. His loss seemed like a relief. I can only guess he did what he did because it was what he felt like he needed to do. He needed to take a stand. He wasn't a politician. He wasn't a businessman. He wasn't an orator or a strategist. But he knew what happened with our schools mattered. Our school was the hub of our community. And he knew that what the leadership of our school system stood for determined the future of our town. He most probably *also* understood that schools fuel communities and communities fuel states and states fuel the country we are proud to call our own. Not the other way around.

We get that concept upside down sometimes.

Dad's example said to me: Start close to home. Do what you can. Let the ripple run.

I think of that when I'm inclined to shrug my shoulders or lift my puzzled palms toward the heavens, as if there's nothing I can do. Whether it be a quandary, a stand-off, or a fear I do not understand—I remember. The problems of our world are so massive. So intricately complex. So deeply rooted in blind generational commitment to hate or loyalty or some other form of epoxy the committed can't even name. It seems so outside of my reach. And yet, the enormity doesn't give me license to not do anything.

Change often starts out itty-bitty. If I can draw a circle around my feet and shore up kindness there, I make a dent. If a group of people can lean in to understanding, pop the cork on grace, and sit for a minute with a belief in their lap that doesn't happen to be their own, then pretty much anything becomes possible. It's not about where we're standing. Or even the size of the thing we're holding in our hands. It's about just doing something. The ripple does the rest.

When I was a kid, my dad would take me pond fishing on the outskirts of town. I fished with a minnow and bobber attached to a Zebco push-button, and he with a spinning reel that tethered a plastic worm. My casts would go about five feet out from the bank (if I was lucky) scarcely clearing the algae where they'd plop in the murky water with a splashy, boisterous *kerplunk*. Dad's toss would whiz out into the far middle of the pond, the hook and lure entering the water seamlessly with a whisper, as if his entire get-up had been invited in. Both of our endgames were the same, but his stature, experience, technical understanding—and thus his tackle—differed from mine.

We both caught fish, though. And both our casts, regardless of presentation, wrinkled the water, creating sweeping circles of their own. Every single time. The size and speed of the undulations set in motion weren't the same, but the ripple always ran.

It's hard to know sometimes where to start when chaos reigns, especially when the knots that need unraveling are wrapped in camouflage or seem so far away. But wherever we are is the mark. A wise man once said, "Let everyone sweep in front of his own door and the whole world will be clean." Such alarmingly simple advice, we struggle to believe it is true.

Start close to home. Do what you can. And let the ripple run.

Help Needed

He came out of nowhere, this long, lanky kid with unkempt curls held back by a thin, elastic band like soccer players wear. "How can I help?" he asked, as my lostness must have been plastered like a billboard on my face.

"Panko breadcrumbs?" I asked, leaving a verbal ellipsis on the end.

"Aisle four," he immediately responded while pointing, "about halfway down on your left. Just below eye level." Then he smiled, "Well, maybe right at eye level for you."

I found them there precisely where he told me they would be, wedged in the middle of the flour and the oats. It would have taken me half a day to find them on my own.

In between the time I entered the store and checked out with my necessities, the young man with messy hair and an athlete's stride had helped an elderly lady who couldn't reach the olives, an associate stocking shelves, a confused middle-aged man trying to maneuver the self-check-out line, and a mother balancing two toddlers and a basket full of food. And that's just what I could see from wherever I happened to be at the time. Who knows how much assistance he provided when out of my line of sight.

The way-finder wearing a red apron was like a human Swiss Army knife—poised and ready to aid whoever was in need. And everything about him said he lived for it. His face lit up like a Christmas tree when he was able to lend a hand. At first glance, he looked to be an ordinary teen who would soon grow tall enough to fit his feet, but upon closer observation, he seemed more like a superhero whose power was a sixth sense for identifying need. The kind that made him a magnet for adding value everywhere he turned.

I once heard a legendary basketball coach say, "Great defenses aren't great because they're good at helping. They're great because they're good at never needing help." While I understand what he was getting at, I never coached a team who could get good at that. It was our mission—always—to guard our yard and not require assistance from a teammate to help us do our jobs. But that was an impossible ask across the board. So, getting better and better at helping was paramount. And becoming proficient at helping whoever helped in the first place was the way we learned we could win.

This ultimately stitched us together. We found great honor in being helpers. What a privilege it is to be what another needs.

We take it for granted sometimes, this capacity we have to make the road a little smoother for those we are traveling with or those we simply shoulder-brush along the way. We either move with our eyes and ears tuned to other channels or we shrug off the signs. Withholding is an easy default when we don't hear anybody ask.

But everybody needs something. We wear an invisible list of what we're missing on a flag across our chests, though mostly we're so busy trying to keep it covered that we don't notice others' similar attire.

My man playing traffic cop just beyond the frozen foods seems to have found a way to see and hear the silent, shrouded cries of, "Help!" And what he gets by responding is the privilege my players felt when they had a chance to rotate on defense and play a role in saving the day.

Helping others fills up holes we don't even know we have.

The sign in the front of the grocery store window reads "Help Wanted," but as I drove away, I wondered if it might behoove the owners to rephrase it as a need. What we desire and what we're thirsting for are often two entirely different things. One comes shrink-wrapped in bravado. The other doesn't come with packaging of any kind, not even a layer of skin. The former is safer than the latter. But the latter is how both parties end up getting what they have to have, which is what they need.

The key ingredient for fried zucchini chips was exactly where aproned Superman said. And he, it seemed, was exactly where I and a store full of shoppers on an accidental Thursday needed him to be. Right place, right time? Maybe. Or maybe circumstances present themselves to those with open eyes.

6

Serendipity

Because of a million things we can't put our finger on, business booms. A relationship crumbles. The tornado turns.

Things happen because they do. We help. We engage. We make choices. We risk time and effort.

Things happen because they don't. We help. We engage. We make choices. We risk time and effort.

We tamper with things, hoping to make a difference to affect the outcome. But we don't always have a say, except to surrender to the inevitable: what is, is.

Que Sera Sera.

We are not in control.

We Stumble

Between the villages of Praiano and Positano on southern Italy's Amalfi Coast, lies a hidden treasure tucked in a cave by the side of the road. It's easy to miss if you don't know it's there and hard to get a look at even if you do. We discovered it on a perilous walk to lunch when we couldn't get a cab.

The work of art, a detailed replica of the city of Praiano, sits at the base of the Grotto del Diavolo (Devil's Cave) along a skinny highway with unforgiving margins, adjacent to the sea. The slight sign flanking it reveals that it is a Nativity scene created by ceramist Michael Castellano. The Nativity is an integral part of Italian culture during Christmas, but also year around. The physical rendering of the city depicts Mary, Joseph, and the crib, but it expands to include the city's churches, markets, brightly colored homes, and cobblestone alleyways. It even depicts the coastline beneath the craggy rock face, with the sea of boats and fishermen below. Ceramic figurines of people going about their daily lives—farming, cooking, carrying, walking—accompany the structures, making it feel as if you're looking at a moment snatched and frozen in time. Jasmine and bougainvillea dot the landscape, lemons drape from trees, birds fly overhead, wine bottles balance on tables, pasta sits on plates. No detail is overlooked. It's as if the artist took a picture and fashioned it in scaled-down 3-D form. The likeness to reality is uncanny. Locals say Castellano continues to add a feature every year.

Sometimes the stuff we stumble on is even better than the stuff we set out to find.

When I turned fifty, my friends gave me a trip to Wimbledon. Tennis had become my later-in-life sports love and my buddies knew. So a group of about ten of us—friends and family—packed our summer whites and flew across the pond to watch Federer and Serena slap tennis balls and to eat strawberries and crème on the lawn.

London, for the record, did not disappoint. We taught ourselves how to navigate the Tube, a process as intriguing as it is an expedient way to travel. We went to St. John's Wood, taking pictures like the Beatles crossing the street at Abbey Road. We walked the Tower Bridge and rode the Eye, hung out on the bank of the Thames and sat awestruck on the stage built by Lord Chamberlain's Men.

But Wimbledon was the main event.

I learned, over the course of several years as a burgeoning tennis aficionado, just enough about strokes and strategy to be dangerous (and annoying). Armed with that and the passionate anticipation I remember from being a little girl who wore my baseball glove on the two-hour car ride from Oklahoma to Texas to take in a Rangers' game, my friends and I packed onto the Tube in route to the English countryside and a slice of another world. As we disembarked at Wimbledon Tennis Club, joining the throng of people walking briskly in their decidedly over-thought-out whites, I felt like a guest at Disneyland. We took before and after pictures at the gate in an attempt to freeze the moment in time.

Wimbledon was amazing. We sat on the front row for men's doubles, watching players we had never heard of blast 100 mph groundies back and forth across the court. We fell for personalities and picked favorites. We sweated through our clothes. Then we went to center court where Serena served aces and Roger charged the net. Everything about it was grand. The tennis, the pageantry, the flowers, the food.

But what I loved most about London turned out to not be the tennis or the Tube or the road where the Beatles became. What I loved most about London was the ice cream I bought in a cone at a tree stand in Hyde Park.

It's not advertised, this obscure hut that sells it. There wasn't even a sign with offerings or prices. The crème de la crème of London was a make-shift counter stuffed between some trees at the turn of a giant field. A place one might unceremoniously trip over if out for an afternoon stroll. They don't have thirty-one flavors and they need you to pay in cash. But when you walk away with a cone in your hand, it's as if all is right with the world.

Bono called these treasures we discover on the way to other things "topline melodies." And he should know as a winner of twenty-two Grammys and leader of the only band in history with a record of number-one hits in the top two-hundred for four consecutive decades. He said the tunes you hear around the corner—the ones that rise above the noise and chatter—are the ones you build your stories on. He continued, "Destiny arrives casually. The melodies we aren't looking for, but simply can't forget, form the trajectory of our lives."

The unplanned, unforgettable prizes we stumble upon feel like lucky addenda—surprises the wind blew in while we were looking the other way. The out-of-nowhere is half the fun. Part of the beauty of topline melodies is that we hardly ever find them. They find us.

Happy Accidents

We used to call our staff meetings "Happy Accidents" because the best stuff almost always happened around all the important stuff I had planned. We tripped over it when our paths crossed, walking in and out of the room.

Small talk in the doorways often led to big ideas. Afterthoughts in the parking lot frequently paved the way to simple solutions that seemed impossible to find inside the room. The edges of our meetings proved more fertile than the middle ever was. All I had to do was call the caucus. Sweet serendipity did the rest.

Our staff met when we needed to discuss things. We met when we needed to re-direct. We met when we needed to come up with something together none of us could devise on our own. We met when I heard the engine sputtering. And we met once every two weeks, whether or not a tangible agenda cried for attention. Something cool could happen if given a random chance.

The spoils and prizes created by human collisions cannot be denied.

We've learned in recent years that virtually all jobs outside of manual labor and the service industry can be done from just about anywhere. Your couch, your backyard, a coffee shop, the beach, the mountains, Australia. Computer screens provide conduits for information, so everything we need is at our fingertips. Literally. And the perks are everywhere. Needy or over-zealous co-workers don't interrupt us, we don't waste time on what to wear, and we don't exchange years of our lives on a two-or four-or six-hour round-trip commute. Technology continues to pinch hit with brilliance. It saved us when we had to have it, and we may never go back to things the way they were. But it's also stolen happenstance.

That might be a shaky trade.

The core of our fan base at women's basketball games at the University of Oklahoma grew from circumstance. Ron's seats were across from John's, who were next to Mary's, who were behind Debbie who was across the aisle from Sue. Now on random weekends, they all go to breakfast together at a place run by another guy who had tickets three rows back. A common cause brought them to the same place at the same time, then serendipity got involved. And now they're all tangled up in each other's grandkids and they know each other's neighbors. That never could have happened had they only watched our games on their TVs.

Sometimes it's not the person, specifically, but simply the interaction with another human that gives serendipity an opening. Maybe you don't become travel buddies or develop a deep symbiotic relationship, but a brief human interaction can open a corridor of thought or knock some things loose inside of you that were stuck and growing stuck-er by the day. When we run into one another, energy is exchanged. Sometimes it's depleted, sometimes it's beefed up. But human encounters create a playground where happy accidents can occur.

We all have people in our lives who we can't remember how we met. It just seems like we've always known them. I can think of five of my favorites right now. Serendipitous friends. People the wind blew in while we were lucky enough to be walking around outside. Sometimes, we wind up in jobs or lifestyles we love but never could have imagined, and we try to trace back *why*. Often, it happened because we went somewhere on a whim and struck up a conversation with a guy who knew a guy who had a place. The next thing we knew, we were buying cattle and ranching had become our way of life. That's sort of how our time on Earth unfurls: we move around, trip and fall on people, things, and places that make us who we are.

Serendipity doesn't discriminate. But it's hard to be the recipient of its graces when we're locked behind a screen. Working via computer from a remote location has value, but it's certainly not a substitute for butting up against one another in the same room. Pixels aren't people. But beyond that - beyond the body language and the warmth of a handshake or a hug, or the feel you get from another person when you're breathing the same air - lies the opportunity that gets created when you simply share a space.

Accidents. We can sometimes help the happy ones happen by calling a meeting whether we need one or not.

The Things That Stick Just Do

Mrs. Davis wore a key on a chain around her neck all day. That's what my adult son remembers about September 11, 2001, of his fourth-grade year. He and his classmates watched movies at school the entire afternoon—with intermittent indoor recess breaks—which he realized was a bit weird, but way too good of a thing to question too intently. He was nine. The novelty felt grand.

This was his teacher's plan, of course. Denise Davis was a five-star if teachers formally were ranked and heralded in such a way. She had a job to do the day two planes flew into the World Trade Center and nobody knew yet why. She was a woman who spoke softly, drew hard lines, and dressed intently for occasions, including ordinary days. My Granny used to say she "looked like she just stepped out of a bandbox" even on playground duty or at an early Saturday morning soccer game in the elements at Griffin Park. So, it makes sense that Colton would notice and remember the way the key hung where her perfectly matched jewelry usually laid.

He can't remember what movies they watched. Or who picked him up from school. Or when and how he discovered what had happened to our world that day while locked inside his classroom.

But the key around his teacher's neck is vivid in his mind.

It's funny the things we can't remember, and the things we can't forget.

When one of my dearest childhood friends lost her father, she asked me to speak at the service. To prepare for my remarks, I asked her what her home address was in the town we grew up in where so many memories were made. I thought the detail would prove poignant.

She had no idea. So she asked her siblings. Then her mother.

No one seemed to know.

"How can it be," she asked incredulously, "that none of us remember the address of the house we called our home?"

"I don't know," I said, as she pulled up 16 Ash Street from the map on Google Earth.

Then she matter-of-factly responded, "I wish I could forget the way he looked when he was sick."

The mind is a marvelous sorter full of boxes, files and drawers. And we have little say about what goes where. We get even less, it seems, about what we can find when we want it, and about what fades away. The things that stick just do.

I can't remember what my mom looked like when she held my first child on the day he was born. I have zero recollection despite my gritty attempts to pull it from the folders in my brain. Yet, I can see—in living color—the giant Snickers bar my brother handed me when they wheeled me back into my room. It was as big around as my wrist, and though it took me a couple of days to do so, I ate every bite. That silly detail sits where I'd prefer my mother's face to be, but for whatever reason, I don't get to make that call.

Frivolous bits of mica get entangled with the moments we'd really like to bronze. It's pretty much a crap shoot which ones will make it the long haul. I don't remember what my daughter's first words were. At the time, I thought I'd never forget so I didn't write them down. But I can still hear the way she said "spasghetti"—the only word, I swear, she ever mispronounced. The highs and lows, the big deals and the not-so-big deals float haphazardly together inside the maze of my mind.

One of the first family trips we took after our granddaughter was born was a trek to the mountains where the air smells like it's been scrubbed and it seems as if you only need to tiptoe to touch the sky. With Austyn in a backpack (on her dad's and then her mom's shoulders, then back on dad's again), we hiked through towering pines. We hopscotched across rolling streams and picnicked on giant flat rocks alongside a river surrounded by jagged snowcapped peaks. I took a million pictures, wanting to remember it all—the green valley where she toddled between the massive walls of rock . . . Aspen leaves that jingled like coins in the plate at church . . . the trees growing out of crooks and crannies that had no imaginable places for roots. Yet even with the photos, it's a stretch for me to truly recall the color of the sky. Few details have stood the test of time.

There is one thing, though, that I cannot forget.

During our trip when it came time for bed, Austyn would want me to accompany her there. "GG, take me," she would say. It was, of course, as if I'd won the lottery every time. One particular night, after giving hugs and running through the obligatory "good nights," "see you laters," and "I love yous," she grabbed my finger and we headed toward the stairs.

Then, "Turn the lights off!" she yelled as a reminder to those not ascending with us.

It is burned into my brain.

It was just a sentence. But its randomness. Her inflection. The way she went from two to twenty as her grown-up recommendation wafted through the air. "Turn the lights off!" stuck in the middle of me.

Like a necklace key or a candy bar or a word that's mispronounced, it became an instant breadcrumb marking a moment made to last.

The things that stick just do.

Near Misses

When Austyn had just learned to wobble-run, she carried her hands like tiny purses in front of her armpits. There, they could function as natural backstops ready to unfurl, protecting her perfect face. The falling was part of the moving. She seemed to get that instinctively. It was the price of doing business in an ambulatory life. Crashing rarely fazed her. She just popped right back up like Gumby and went on her way again. I was the one on pins and needles. Daily, I would jolt, typically too late and too far away to prevent potential disaster, but on call, nonetheless. Miracles of near misses punctuated my day. She wobbled on, oblivious.

Most of us keep a basket full of "what ifs" on a shelf within arm's reach. It's our inherent right that we seem to deem a privilege as human beings, to borrow trouble and keep a working list of ways to worry about what might be. Rightly so. The world is full of precarious corners. It's a wonder any of us make it to the end of any day. The miracle of the miracles we forget to count.

Bad stuff happens. Awful, horrible stuff. But mostly it doesn't. Not when compared to what could. We pass through an intersection just milliseconds before a car barrels through the stop sign right behind where we just were. The tornado picks back up into the sky a quarter mile from our house. The scissors we drop don't land on our toe. The fall we take doesn't end in a break. We dodge bullets all the time. But we struggle to put our near misses in the count-your-blessings bag.

Life moves, with most of its crooks and turns untraceable to a cause and an effect. Things just happen. And they don't. Our Boy Scout/ Girl Scout blood curdles at the realization that we don't have much control.

As a coach, injuries were the unpredictable havoc-wrecker on a season. In a sport like basketball, with such a small roster, the absence of one athlete lost to injury from the line-up changes everything within a flash. When one of our players would get hurt, upending our season, the first place everyone's brain went to visit was Explanation Land. *Why did this have to happen? What did I do? What am I missing that this unfortunate occurrence is forcing me to find?*

It's as if filling in the blanks with reason and purpose could make a bad thing worth its while. Players would sometimes unpack events backward. "If I had just shot it when I was open instead of driving it . . . If I had only worked on my hamstrings . . . I should have stretched more before the game . . ." Coaches do it, too. "If we just hadn't done the last rep of that drill. . .If we practiced lighter the day before, then her quad wouldn't have been so fatigued . . . Why did I call that lob play, anyway?"

We want there to be a rational reason. A place to place blame. Our humanness aches for tangible logic. If we could just connect the dots, perhaps we could keep some of the bad stuff at bay.

In an attempt to avoid the rabbit hole, my team and I created a "go-to" mantra when we found ourselves tempted to ask, "Why me?" to all the bad. We countered it with "Why me?" to all the good. It was a quick re-calibrator for woe-is-me. We made a list of the myriad of not-so-great things that could have happened, but for whatever reason, never did. Like why didn't Roz's non-ACL-knee ever completely blow out? Or why didn't Courtney ever sprain an ankle? Not everything can be understood.

We don't naturally collect and catalog near misses. Negative impressions can be extremely hard to hold. But they still play important, defining roles. And they are EVERYWHERE. We escape all kinds of close encounters every single day. The big ones go in a but-for-the-grace-of-God crate we store in the top of the closet, while the *common* ones dissipate mostly without fanfare or recall.

Three weeks after our first child was born, my husband rolled the Jeep he was driving down a rural road on his way to work. Both the tightly fastened seat belt and his clinched grip on the steering wheel kept him inside of the vehicle that had no top until it finally landed upright on four wheels. But at the age of twenty-eight, he had a broken neck.

That happened, yet so much else didn't.

A few days after the accident he walked into the neurosurgeon's office to get checked out because his head started feeling heavy. It made him the first one of Dr. Stewart Smith's patients, with this particular set of vertebrae compressions, to ever walk into his office on their own two feet. After a complicated surgery and a rather pesky rehab, Dane was good as new.

I wondered. I still wonder. Did he tuck his chin in at just the right time? Were his overdeveloped baseball shoulders responsible for the save? What kept the shattered fragments of his spinal cord from shooting out in every direction, rendering him paralyzed? What made them form a pile, instead, that a gifted neurosurgeon could remove? The list of all that happened couldn't touch the list of all that did not. The blessings came in buckets with tags that read, "Near Miss."

When Austyn first tried to walk, she preferred the driveway to the grass, and the downhill-uphill slopes of concrete to the plentiful stretches of level surface where I preferred she play. I lived on red alert. As I scurried always just a reach away—ahead, behind, beside—of this Weeble in constant motion, I marveled at how many times a day we had *almosts*.

Almosts that disappeared as suddenly as they happened. They just blended in with the treasures she dug up inside the cement cracks. Additions we add to the list of marvelous wonders in our unpredictable lives.

7
No Points for Pretty

Learning is messy. We like to think it's a straight line gradually rising toward the sky. Two steps forward. Two steps forward. Two steps forward. Upward and onward, like the yodeling mountain climber on the game show "The Price is Right."

Except we know from experience that isn't true. Learning is two steps forward, one step back, slide down a hole, climb up again, slip, forward march, crawl a bit . . .

A graph of it would look like the crayon scribbles of a toddler.

When asked how he worked, Einstein answered resolutely, "I grope." In other words, he tried things, which didn't always turn out well. With blind uncertainty, he chased his curiosity wherever it led.

Squiggly lines map the way.

Gorilla Glue

For as long as I can remember, I have been enamored with Curious George. Our local library had a film series my Granny took me to every Friday. We diminutives sat, feet dangling, on grown- up plastic chairs in front of a painted cinder wall where the cartoon came to life, spurring our imaginations and driving our orneriness. My heart skipped a beat every time the clickety-clop of the projector signaled the arrival of that funny little monkey. I can't remember if there was music or even what the narrator's voice sounded like. But I can still hear the crackling of the film as I sat with bated breath, waiting for the man in the yellow hat to stride across the screen, smooth the ruffled edges and save George from himself.

I loved all of George's adventures. The one where he kept calling the firemen, the one where he couldn't say no to the balloons, the one where he was supposed to be delivering newspapers, but just couldn't resist making them into boats to float down the stream at the park. He was always up to something. I knew, as we all did, trouble was not far down the road. Even for a five-year- old, the impending chaos of reality was fairly easy to see. That's what we watched for, the mess he could make out of nothing. His unwillingness to obey often made me, the "rule-follower", antsy. Nonetheless, I loved to watch his wide eyes question the newness of his world. George drew you in with his innocence, but without his vaudeville quizzical nature, he was just a cute monkey. His curiosity was the quicksand that sucked us in and kept us coming back for more.

No matter how full and multi-dimensional George was, without the flatness of the man in the yellow hat, the stories never would have worked. The guy was so flat he didn't even have a name. He was smart, predictably so, and he was kind. But beyond that, the man in the yellow hat didn't have much going on. He merely slipped in and out to cage the monkey tales without getting in the way. Essential, but not sticky. You slid right off him.

Hanging out with George, however, was like walking through a spider web.

I think I would have loved to have had George, the ornery monkey, on my team. He was never "just okay" with much of anything. Neutral was not his happy place. He craved to know why, when, where and how. And what else, what else, what else! Athletes with that kind of unfettered curiosity don't just move the ball down the field, they move the goal line. Their infectious digging changes the game for all involved.

For coaches, the questions from truly curious athletes are oxygen. Their seeking enhances our understanding. It clears out the corners of hard-to-reach places, making us better at what we do while simultaneously reminding us of all we love about it. I once had a point guard who showed up at my office early on mornings following a game. She wanted to watch the film to see what she missed. Or could have done better. Or should have looked at to make a different play. She didn't do it to revel in her ESPN SportsCenter moments—though she often did, as there were plenty. She didn't do it to stick a figurative pencil in her eye for a missed wide-open lay-up or a pass she threw to the other team. She did it because she was curious. She wanted to understand the game. Breathing together, we would forage.

Curious players are stick-um for their teams. Teammates find another level of commitment when they know their receiver's brother's name, and that he likes fishing in his free time, more than anything. The connection between a point guard and a post player becomes symbiotic. In one respect, it's because of the reps and the skill. But it's also because of the human-being knowledge that you get when spending time together asking questions about one another's life. It's as if when you know her favorite song, you can feel where to throw her the ball. Or if she knows what you loved most about your grandmother, you can catch anything she tosses your way. You can feel the glue forming in your fingers, on your soul.

Children are special bastions of curiosity. "Daddy," a young one asks, "why is the sky blue?"

"Because the ions bounce off the sun and blue light waves are shorter than others," answers Dad, whose Discovery Channel obsession prompts Mom, who is the reader, to get involved.

"That's not exactly right," she counters. Then the real talk ensues.

Digression goes to sunsets, water molecules, and the role gases play in the atmosphere. Eventually, the case is tried by Google, and everybody learns something—even if it's something they knew but forgot. The one-off is that you're reminded what a great team you make as you sludge through the stuff you're just not sure of. The goose-chase sticks you together.

I have a friend whose daughter recently asked, "Mom, when I pray, why do I have to say 'amen' at the end? Why can't I say, 'A girl?' I mean, I'm a girl. What does 'amen' even mean, anyway?"

"Well," her careful and compassionate mother responded, "'Amen' actually means 'so be it' so you're really just saying at the end of your prayer, 'God, go ahead and do your thing.' So, no, I guess you don't have to say 'amen.' You can say anything you want, really. It's your prayer after all."

To which her daughter thoughtfully responded, "I'm gonna say 'a girl.' That's what I'm gonna do when I'm done talkin' to God."

And so, she does. (Don't you know God gets a kick outta her.) Healthy doubt is essential to growth. It's how, despite our age, we learn to figure things out.

Everything George, the curious monkey, encountered was new. Every experience was a first for him, so there was no confining mold. And all of us who watched or read about George were given the gift of learning to look through a diamond-shaped window in the house's corner, instead of falling into the trap of looking through the boring and predictable front door.

Sometimes as teachers and parents, we think we're supposed to have all the answers. But I'm not sure that's our most important job. Maybe we'd be better served to pose the questions and fade into the background as subtle safety patrol while those for whom we are responsible twist and squirm and learn. Like George and the foil who made him famous—the man in the yellow hat.

I have a deep affinity for people who ponder, especially out loud. Digging gets us dirty, in binds, and in need of help—often to get out of a mess we made because we couldn't help ourselves. But that's how the wrinkles of experience get carved.

I worry about a world that hasn't time for wondering, for head-scratching, for pursed lips and hair twisting. Nobody ever pondered better than Curious George.

To this day, when I walk into the public library, I breathe in and think of George. The smell of cold books sandwiched between tin shelves reminds me of all I used to wonder about and all I still don't know.

Sweet Spot

What would you do if nobody paid you for it? Would you still sell houses, or work on cars, or do people's taxes, or deliver the news?

Would you coach ball, or drive a tractor, or teach a class, or build a boat? When your feet hit the floor in the morning, where is it that your heart can't wait to go?

If you followed it where it led you, you might end up where you already are. You might find yourself some place entirely different. Some place you've never been or imagined you might go. But the corner you'll find yourself in, if you chase the song in your heart, is what I believe is your sweet spot. The place where all kinds of good collides.

If you've ever hit a golf ball clean, you know what the sweet spot feels like. It's soft, yet solid, and it's coated in sticky comeback juice. Despite the effortlessness of the cut, the ball soars on invisible wings, and all you hear in your head once you hit it, is, "I can't wait to do that again." That's part of the magic that lives in the sweet spot. Being there never gets old.

A fun and often trendy dinnertime conversation topic is what we might do if we won the lottery. If a sack of money the size of five lifetimes fell out of the sky into our lap, what would we do with it? Nearly everybody says, first, they'd give a lot away. That's who we hope we are. We name the charity we'd give a windfall to or the foundation we would start. And then . . . we would build a house here and buy a house there and we'd go somewhere exotic at least once a year. We'd buy tickets to every major sporting championship, buy our parents long-term care insurance, our kids new cars, and, of course, we'd quit our jobs.

But then what? What would we DO?

Doing nothing is only fabulous when it's done as a reprieve. Running around being busy is not the point of life, but we're not built to lounge on the beach all day, regardless of the breathtaking views. We are created to contribute. We come out of the womb wired to work. "The pitcher cries for water to carry," wrote the poet, Marge Piercy, "and a person for work that is real." We were born to be of use, to serve a purpose. But the conundrum we sometimes wrestle with is *how*.

I used to tell my players to follow what they were good at until it ran into what they loved. The intersection would be their sweet spot, the place where they would thrive. But they often got snagged on the rough edges. There were always pieces of the whole that didn't intrigue them. "Teachers have to grade papers," they'd say. "Lawyers have to do research. I want to do something where I don't have to do math."

Even fun isn't fun all the time, I'd remind them. The point is what endures. After the annoyances (that part of the work you would like to live without) are gone, what remains? Does the spring in your step hang around? Non-stop enjoyment doesn't equal fulfillment. Enjoyment is thin and flighty. Fulfillment is way sturdier. It doesn't dissipate. Sometimes work isn't fun, even when it's work you were born to do. But the enduring kind, the soul-stirring kind, will fuel you long after it's done, regardless of who sees or hears it, or how much somebody compensated you to do it. In the sweet spot, the heart continues to swell.

We have so many options when it comes to choosing the work that we do. Unfortunately, a lot of time is spent obsessing over absolutes. "What am I *meant* to do? What *could* I do? What *should* I do?" The sweet spot doesn't come to you while you wring your hands. You go find it. Like a shopper at a sale rack, you explore. And the more you try, the more you'll know. By doing lots of different things, you learn to recognize what strikes the band in your heart. That sound, once you learn to hear it, will almost always lead you home.

Patchwork Pillows

In the fourth grade, I learned how to sew a pillow. We did it in class. Parents were livid. They didn't believe we were *learning*.

Mrs. Henderson, our teacher, had long, dark, thick and shiny hair that looked as if she brushed it one hundred strokes at night. She wore bright clothes and a headband—not around like a hippie might, but up and back the way a cover girl would. She taught us stuff. How to make a patchwork pillow is what I remember most.

She also read *Old Yeller* aloud (southern accents and all) every day at 2:00 p.m., about thirty minutes before the final bell. Back then, there was no PETA to censor a book about the killing of a dog. If there was, nobody talked about it. Especially in a rural school that people only stumble upon if they make a wrong turn when they exit off the highway. I'm grateful PETA stayed out of it, too. Because if they'd been around, I might not have met *Old Yeller* and that would have been a travesty. I loved the Coates family. I loved their dog. And I loved that no worksheets accompanied the reading. We just listened to our teacher read a story about a stray yellow pup, then we got to make of it what we would.

It was there in Mrs. Henderson's classroom that I first learned about foreshadowing. Though I wasn't aware of it then. Our teacher would peer over the top of the golden hardback book, pausing strategically for effect when she came to the parts that hinted at the dog's ultimate, unfortunate demise. When she came to the detailed account of Old Yeller's violent tussle with the wild-eyed wolf, we all knew something important was coming. She taught us to look for it with her giant brown eyes.

Mrs. Henderson read without distraction. (Which I found remarkable given the audience.) She read with rhythm and feeling. She read with dialect. She read with style. And when she got to the part about necessity—the part where Travis, the oldest brother, did what he had to do—her throat tightened, and she couldn't read on. So, she asked me to come up to do what she couldn't. I got to read the last three pages of *Old Yeller* to the room.

Mrs. Henderson rose from her chair, handed me the book, and slid quickly to the back to join my classmates sitting cross-legged on the floor. She grabbed a tissue and let me be Travis doing grown-up work, protecting mama and Arliss while Mr. Coates was away from the farm. I didn't have to shoot Old Yeller, but I got to slip on responsibility and wear it in front of my friends.

Don't try to convince me learning didn't happen inside Mrs. Henderson's room. We learned because she let us. She threw real life out into the middle of the floor and then got out of the way.

What my fourth-grade teacher did better than any teacher I ever had, was put everything in a bowl and stir it around with a stick—some sewing, some cooking, some reading, a whole lot of math. We grew plants (to learn about science) in plastic cups lined neatly along the window ledge. We wrote letters to famous people (to learn about history) and picked up trash (to learn about service) from the playground on sunny spring days. In Mrs. Henderson's classroom, the curriculum was part of the patchwork pillow—a piece, but not the whole of what she set out to teach us every day. She recognized the importance of basics, for sure, but she wanted us to be more than regurgitating robots. She wanted us to learn how to do things. How to think, how to live.

It didn't always work out perfectly, though, this unconventional approach to education. Sometimes the stirring got a little messy and spilled over the edge. There was a lot going on inside her classroom.

I remember a semi-stink that arose one time about how Mrs. Henderson spelled *potato* on a sign. Apparently, she added the *e* like you do when it goes plural. It was on a wooden easel in the corner of her room, unexpectedly visible to visitors on the night of Open House. Some parents' britches popped. I think my folks just rolled their eyes. But in our teacher's defense, I could see where the confusion could have come from. Our language has some interesting spelling laws. Why wouldn't potato end with an *e*? Why shouldn't you just add an *s* to make it plural? *E* sometimes belongs and sometimes it doesn't. It can get tough to keep up with, especially in a sea of patchwork sewing with a mini-nursery on the shelf. Truth be known, I think a lot of people were unsure about how to spell the word. I remember a great deal of ciphering going on in the hall.

It didn't faze those of us in Mrs. Henderson's class, though. The next day she simply drew a line through the *e* and kept on going. Kind of like she told us to do when we messed up. Funny thing is, I never forgot how to spell potato. Or tomato. As it turned out, the *e* was a fairly easy thing for an educated person to be confused about. Dan Quayle, the former Vice President of the United States, did it on national television in 1992.

Perfect teachers were not what a bunch of nine-year-olds needed. What we needed was information and instruction, space for exploration, guidance about how to do practical things, and examples of how to handle missteps. We needed the balance of it all—the pillows, the spelling, the imperfection.

I hated it when fourth grade had to end.

I felt like such a grown-up inside that chamber piped with independent air, the one with the tag on the door that read, "Mrs. Henderson's Room." Even though it may have seemed unorthodox to outsiders, inside her walls, school made perfect sense. The dots of the *what* and the *why* were connected by a squiggly line.

That patchwork pillow I made in her class stayed with me for years. Decades even. Not because it was particularly pretty, but because it stood for something I didn't want to throw away. It smelled, looked and felt like learning. The kind that lasts forever, no matter what you do.

8

Growing Pangs

So much unknown looms.

When who we were no longer fits, and the chasm between where we are and where we want to be is wide, standing on the precipice can be scary.

The blurry *in-between* sometimes compels us to dig in, making *safely stuck* somehow seem a better choice than *letting go*.

Stretching can leave marks. Battle scars, some call them. Badges that reflect a tough thing lived through.

The call to increase, expand, improve, progress typically comes laced with apprehension, and yet, who among us wants to just stay where we are?

Homesick

It hit me from out of nowhere the summer after I turned ten . . .

The Lindsey All-Star Camp brochure had been lying on our kitchen counter for months. It was a full-color, tri-fold production with a picture of its founder, Charlie Heatly, on the front. Inside it had a sample daily schedule, some pictures of coaching headliners, and an aerial shot of a gym full of ambitious campers dribbling in unison in matching white camp T-shirts with their respective last names ironed across the back. The portion of the brochure below the dotted line where you filled out your personal information had been clipped and sent in with a check only days after the opportunity had arrived in the mail. I looked at it, minus its entry form, every single day for months. I could not wait to go.

I'd been packing for my week away for weeks before departure, even though the essentials were all that were essential for an eight-in-the-morning-to-eight-at-night daily gymnasium grind. I laid out shorts, shoes, travel-size soap and shampoo, toothpaste, toothbrush, towels, a set of twin-bed sheets, a blanket, a pillow and lots and lots and lots of socks. Then I laid awake at night dreaming of June.

When the day circled in red on the calendar finally arrived, I couldn't get to basketball camp fast enough. Once there, my mom helped me get checked-in and find my assigned room in the hallway of middle-school classrooms that masqueraded in the summers as a hotel. Then she helped me make my bed (aka mattress lined up on the tile floor side by the side of twenty others) as I hurriedly slipped on my hot-off-the-press camp T-shirt and laced up my canvas Chucks.

We said our goodbyes quickly, half-hugged in the street for good measure, and I bounded up the steps outside the gymnasium toward the serenading whistle of Sweet Georgia Brown. All the stars had most certainly aligned. I had everything I wanted. I was living my best life. Then my mom drove away, and I thought I might die.

It hit me like a tsunami.

I was exactly where I'd dreamed of being and yet, suddenly, I wanted to be anywhere but there. My heart weighed a thousand pounds. It was as if, despite my careful packing, I'd left part of me at home. Prior to that moment, I'd never really known anything other than happy, sad, and mad—with the latter two of those three being emotional visitors who only briefly came and went. But there, alone in a crowded gymnasium, I experienced a seismic shift. I was paralyzed by a yearning.

It wasn't my mom, per se, or our house or my room that I missed. It was all of it. I was sick for *home*. I ached for all that was familiar that I could no longer reach out and touch. I could feel myself floating, untethered. Blind-sided. Dizzy with emotion, not sure which way was up.

That's how homesickness happens. It buries you alive in waves.

While my first encounter with the malady came when I was ten, it's kept up a steady appearance through the years. I felt it again when I moved into my dorm at college. And again, several years later, when I moved away from campus with a diploma in my hand. It washed over me when Dane and I sold our first house . . . and again when I first took the kids to school . . . and again twelve and sixteen years later, respectively, when each one got their own formal graduation papers and moved out from under our roof.

I feel it sometimes still when the congregation sings "I'll Fly Away" at church, and when I pull weeds from the well at the base of a newly planted tree (the way my dad once taught me to). I feel it when I put my Christmas decorations away, and when I travel (almost always, regardless of where I go) and at the first cool smell of fall.

The sand siphons out from below my feet and I go under.

I get sick for home. A place I can feel in my bones that I can't get to.

Some might call this nostalgia, but homesickness is needier than that. It's a bottomless pit of melancholy minus the fangs of grief. And the worst part about this disease of displacement is that even when you feel it coming, there's no way to escape. It's like restless leg syndrome of the heart. You can't ignore it and yet there's not much of anything you can do to make it go away. Half of you— or what you love (which is often the very same thing)—is here and half is somewhere else. No matter how you contort, you cannot fill the void.

They say when a tsunami is coming, if you find yourself in a boat, the best thing to do is head out to sea. It's the running away that will drown you. As I've gotten older, I've learned to not try so hard to hang on. I just let the feeling overtake me, relishing and re-living everything I miss. I still get out of breath and a little scared when it hits, but letting it do what it's bound to do anyway somehow makes me feel less upside down. Homesickness is, after all, despite its heavy shroud, a reminder of the good gone missing. A hole only appears where a thing of substance used to be.

Big Shoes

Little feet can't resist big shoes. Austyn is closer to two than she is to one and nothing is more attractive to her than an empty pair of grown-up sneakers—especially her mom's. She's determined, too. She'll work with the focus of a surgeon to slide her feet underneath the laces and then willfully scoot around. Danger is at every turn in the giant kicks that are almost the length of her tiny leg, and yet she doesn't seem to notice or to care. It's as if whatever risk is there is worth it. She will not be deterred. What she wants is to be what she feels like she is when she wears her mama's shoes. BIG.

It's what we all think we want until we are.

When I held the corner office at the women's basketball complex at OU, I often received various kinds of letters from aspiring coaches. About every third one of them said, "I want to know how to get a job like yours, a job where all I do is coach ball. I hate dealing with all this other stuff."

I'd answer them with the gospel truth, "You don't want my job then."

The basketball was buried so deep underneath the "other stuff" that getting to the court most days was like a giant game of *Where's Waldo*. Things that *had* to be done were woven into and around all the things I longed to do. And most of them were hard.

It's easy to watch Nick Saban run out of the tunnel from inside a giant plume of smoke and want to be *big* like him someday. As you watch him in his one-ear headphones from your 50-yard line seat, what you cannot see is his to-do list, or the piles in his office that have spilled from his desk to the credenza to the floor, or the invisible backpack he is wearing full of other people's ills. The ball is the work that only works if the other stuff gets done.

That's the trick about growing up. The fun balloons come with strings attached to things that aren't that fun. CEOs know. So do presidents, small business owners, coaches, teachers, and parents. While big shoes look alluring from a distance, they're not that easy to wear.

Little people, however, do not care. Big is their nirvana. They can't wait to be like the towers that pick them up and swing them around. They want to drive cars . . . make money . . . sleep wherever they want. From where they're standing, little looks as lovely as the spoils that come from being big.

So it's imperative that we learn to balance our load. Though a lot of "heavy" comes with getting older, that doesn't mean age has to swallow up fun.

My favorite scene from the movie *Big* is when Josh (Tom Hanks), a little boy who wants to be "big," gets his wish granted. He walks, in a grown-up body, wistfully through his old neighborhood as a man who missed the middle. Josh watches his friends boldly ride their bikes, play in enormous piles of leaves, take a goofy class picture in front of the school, play baseball in the local park, and he aches to be unencumbered. He pines for laughter and friendships that aren't so complicated by imperceptible grown-up rules. The boy he was—the one buried beneath the external entrapments of his tricked-out apartment and his uber-successful life—is still inside. Josh wants to set him free. He yearns for the simple joy of simply being a kid.

It's hard not to miss that innocence when taxed with being big.

The adults Josh found himself surrounded by lived burdened. And yet, every person he interacted with lightened up because the inner child in *him* rubbed off on them. As they were reminded of who they used to be, a forgotten joy emerged.

My granddaughter gets this look on her face when she sees her mom's shoes. It's a mixture of mischief and confidence as she beelines toward them with purpose in her eyes. I think she likes the lure of the shoes and the challenge of moving around successfully in them. But I think she likes being like her mama even more.

That's what we can't afford to forget. Little ones are always watching how we wear big shoes.

Rigor

"We do not apologize for our rigor here." That's how the president welcomes parents on day one to new-student orientation at Carnegie Mellon University. Can't you just hear a British accent dripping off a baritone voice? If you're one of the exemplary 15% of high school applicants who gets an opportunity to attend there, sleep better not be high on your priority list. And if you're the parent of a student about to embark on the journey, you best leave your helicopter at home. They aren't messing around. There's no opening joke. There's no awkward drivel about the history of the place. No "Welcome! Welcome! Congratulations for producing such a prodigious child!" Just a clear-cut, "You'd better get ready." A straightforward lay of the land.

I pulled my shoulders back and sat up taller in my chair when I heard the story. I can't imagine how the parents in the room must have felt. An unapologetic promise of rigor. I didn't know people made those anymore. Expectations not encased by bubble wrap.

What a gift! In one succinct sentence, the parents in attendance were served notice for how things were going to go. They were given a frame for the next four years of their children's lives, a spandex one that would stretch to contain whatever it might need to hold. Ironically, the rigor in the middle of the *what, when,* and *where* would be what would change the shape of things.

Immovable hard is like that. It makes our insides grow.

When people ask me to talk about my favorite moments from coaching, one that comes to mind is a road trip to Lawrence, Kansas during the pandemic year. The game is tattooed on my soul.

In 2020, we all found ourselves at the base of a mountain we did not sign up to climb. COVID-19 popped up like a monolith in the middle of the freeway while we were all going one-hundred miles an hour with our eyes everywhere but on the road. We ran into it with our faces. What happened next was a bunch of really hard things. For college athletes and coaches, the global pandemic meant (among many other things) trying to run and play or teach and coach basketball in masks. It also meant trying to communicate and unite and fight and scratch and claw and sweat without touching—a concept as weird as it was challenging. In addition, the rules surrounding play throughout the pandemic changed almost daily and most all of them contradicted one another. It was like walking through a giant haunted house with scary half-arms and chains mauling at us from the periphery while monsters were leaping out of the corners at every turn. You never knew what was coming.

Lawrence, Kansas—it was the hardest part of a very hard season that I remember most.

We had nine players on our roster going into the asterisk year after opt-outs and injuries were factored in, but we were committed to piecing the year together. The NCAA allowed conferences to do what they needed to get their games in, so in the Big 12 conference, league play started prior to Christmas. In early December we opened on the road at Kansas, but we entered the hall of horrors on the day before we left.

In the days of the lock-down season, we had a cotton swab stuffed up our nose every single morning. About an hour of purgatory followed as we waited for the results to come back about who could and could not play. On the day we were to depart for Lawrence, about an hour after testing, I got the call that one of our point guards tested positive. This set contact-tracing into motion. It was also determined that our leading scorer, her roommate, had been within striking distance and as such she, too, was not allowed to play. That knocked us down to seven. Our trainers then began combing through practice film, attempting to determine whether anyone else was compromised. One coach was sidelined because she had watched film with the player who tested positive. One manager was quarantined because he shared dinner with her. We had what we had so we ducked our heads and started to map out a way to win.

About fifteen minutes into the conversation, our trainer came in with more bad news.

Our post player had wrapped Christmas presents with the point guard—she was out, too. Uh-oh. We were down to six. We thought the threshold for competition was seven players, but the conference office reminded us that even though the rule read "six scholarship players," it did not say "six players total." There was no addendum. We needed to play. As I gathered the staff, I got the call that our strength coach tested "inconclusive." That news meant another pre-game change and fewer hands-on deck. We took a deep breath, walked through a new defensive strategy, and added a couple of offensive wrinkles for the way we would have to play.

Then we were off to Kansas, my determined band of ballers and me with *Maybe* on our minds.

We took the floor at Phog Allen Fieldhouse, fought our guts out with six (four freshmen, no post, and zero experience at point guard) and we had the lead as we entered the last four minutes of the game. Unfortunately, a couple of critical turnovers down the stretch did us in. One player who had been precariously playing with four fouls finally fouled out. We ended the game with the five we had who were still allowed to play, and when the final buzzer blew and Kansas had more points than we did, our six raced off the floor to fall apart.

Audible sobs filled the post-game locker room. The kind that come from some place deep inside you that you didn't know you had. Our six were shattered. I tried to tell them that as bad as the devastation felt, it would be good in a forever kind of way. This is what it feels like, I told them, when you throw your whole heart in the ring. Knowing you can do that will change the course of your lives. I told them that they would grow more from their valiant fighting that night than from any other single thing that might happen that year, regardless of the numbers glowing in Allen Fieldhouse displaying the final score.

The difficulty of the undertaking made our insides double in size.

I didn't like the way the game ended any more than my players did, but I've never been prouder of a group. It's one of my favorite memories from a file full of twenty-five years. The forty-eight-hour gauntlet gave us walls to run into that would shape what we could become.

I hope Carnegie Mellon never apologizes for the rigor. As a matter of fact, I hope they put their promise on a billboard and shine lights on it at night. I've never known anything better for getting things to grow.

9

Potholes

Most experiences come with speed bumps, unintentional detours, and stretches of time when our feet—like Fred Flintstone's in his car before takeoff—run 'round and 'round in place.

Hardly anything happens without a hitch.

But that doesn't mean everything is hard. Sometimes things are just complicated. Or confusing. Or fly-at-a-picnic annoying. Commotion is a given.

Always Something

"Bad things come in threes," Granny always said. If the washing machine breaks down, you can probably count on the air conditioner going out. And when the air conditioner goes out, you better check on the spare tire in the trunk—a flat very well might be just around the bend. I don't know if she or any of us ever believed it. All superstitions feel kinda hokey to me. But it *did* happen a lot. Looking back, it seems like the rule-of-three was more of an organizational tool used for coping than it was a rule of thumb. A way of putting brackets around things so we felt like we were in the clear for a while. But the truth of the matter is things just go awry.

It's always something.

Sometimes I wonder if God switched on the waves on the sixth night, right before the day he rested. Like maybe he knew floating would only be fun for a bit, so he set the dial on churn. Choppy water does make better sailors. Maybe he was trying to keep us on our toes.

I don't know about you, but my God-given calves have all kinds of muscles from walking around on pointe.

Philosopher Friedrich Nietzsche (1844-1900) came up with a phrase for how to best deal with the constant undulation of life. His suggestion was to love it. Love it all—the good, the bad, the hiccups, the burps. Nietzsche proposed that we wrap our arms around the entire spectrum. "Amor fati," he wrote in Latin. Love your fate! It was his formula for human wisdom. What a beautiful, noble, centered way to live.

Too bad he went mad before he turned sixty.

Loving it all, while a brilliant and noble aspiration, is a reach test most of us fail to pass. Amor fati is not an easy thing to do. The concept is a pillar of stoicism (a mindset shift that is currently enjoying a renaissance in our country), but it reads a little easier than it lives. It's a GREAT idea. And if you can do it, it's a wildly advantageous way to travel through your days. But it can be a challenge.

Especially when it comes to pesky things.

Like mosquitoes. And armadillos. And faulty sprinkler heads. And screws that strip . . . spills that stain . . . people who keep their eyes peeled for a chance to make a stink.

There's always going to be something that can nudge you off your mark.

Laura Numeroff is a best-selling children's author who has a whole series of books built on the concept of potential angst. It all started with a mouse who was given a cookie and then asked for a glass of milk . . . then a straw . . . then a napkin . . . then a mirror. The mouse ultimately ends up thirsty, asks for a glass of milk, and—of course—wants a cookie to go with it. A series of "always somethings" lead to messes that boomerang *right back* to the original something.

The domino effect of inconveniences was so relatable that Numeroff kept going. What would happen if you took a mouse to a movie or to school or gave it a brownie? The idea hit such a bull's-eye that it spilled over to a moose and a muffin, a dog and a donut, and a pig and a pancake. It seems there just is no hard stop for messy stuff that happens.

Vexing things to trip on can pop up almost anywhere.

For reasons that don't seem to make much sense, we're often able to wrestle the big bad stuff that happens into purpose. We can find the silver lining. We can "make the mess our message." It's the milk-spills where we tend to slip and fall.

When my friend, Dru, was going through chemo, she returned home after a long weekend away just in time for an uncharacteristic November thunderstorm to uproot a giant tree from her front yard and sling it across the driveway. She texted me a picture of the aftermath with a caption: "Oh well. It's always something."

Yes, it is.

Sometimes the thing that comes down the pike is big and hairy and it has to be stared down. But most of the time it's just irksome. The 'something' is more like a hangnail or a piece of bacon that's stuck between your teeth. Or a drawer handle that falls off about every third time you pull it. It's simply stuff you have to deal with that you hadn't factored in.

Where you're standing has much to do with how things look. The wrinkles, the rocks in the road, the things that require a deep breath before we tackle them, they're at every turn. The sobering reality of most jobs, and of life, is not whether something's lurking around the corner. It's how you handle what's lurking around the corner when it comes.

Sideways

Recently, Austyn and I had a sleepover. On these fantastic every-once-in-a-whiles, we pile into the bed in Chandler's old room, watch a few episodes of Cocomelon, and tell stories over and over in the dark. When morning comes, she always exclaims, "It's wake-up time!" This signals our pilgrimage down the hall to start the day. We roll out from under the covers, land our feet on the hardwood floor and like a couple of wobbly newborn colts we make our way.

"We're walking funny, aren't we?" I asked rhetorically, as Austyn in my yellow Lakers T-shirt teetered her way unsteadily half-a-step ahead of me.

"GG, this is crazy. I'm like walking sideways," she said, her eyebrows high in the middle, her lips pursed together in a perplexed sort of bow.

I chuckled while reaching to smooth her bed-head hair that now extended below her shoulder blades. Sideways was not at all the track she intended. And yet, that was the way her body on autopilot had decided it would go.

"Who among us hasn't been *there*?" I thought, recognizing the tilt. Spinning off without our own approval. Skidding haplessly in a direction that doesn't seem to serve our purpose. Crossways, perpendicular to the path.

Despite our best intentions, sometimes it's just insanely hard to walk a line.

I've spent a substantial part of my life immersed in competitive sports. Our teams rarely took the floor without a plan, and though I'd like to say we always followed it to a T, that would not be true. We knew what we wanted to do, how we wanted to do it. The road was clear, at least inside our practice minds. Yet, there came a point (more often than I'd like to admit) when things would start to spin off. The ball would be moving . . . the players performing the tasks they had been assigned . . . the score dutifully taking care of itself. Then suddenly, off the rails we'd go. And nobody could quite say why. The ball would start to stick, cuts would morph from tight to loopy, the carefully choreographed dance would stutter on its way to breaking down. Then the score, in valiant predictability, would reflect the lateral lean.

Sometimes we could course-correct, occasionally we couldn't. Invariably though, when the contest was over, we'd look back at the skid often being able to pinpoint precisely where and when it happened. The riddle we had trouble solving wasn't where and when, but how.

You don't see sideways coming. It just does.

Like lightning leaving a burn mark, a text message arrives void of tone, and off we go. A comment gets taken out of context, and we bend. A slight lands without a directed arrow, but painfully in a soft spot just the same. And as quickly as a wet bar of soap squirts out of purposeful hands, whatever we were sure about is gone. We look around and don't know what upright is. When we get sideways with those we care about, the pieces don't seem to fit.

But mostly, things go askew less loudly. There is no emphatic explosion. No sirens sound and no one marks the spot. Our steps just start to veer off-kilter. Sometimes the ground changes grade ever so slightly underfoot. Sometimes the climate shifts, the air swelling a bit thicker overhead. Sometimes a pleasant breeze turns into a distracting wind. And sometimes, for no palpable reason we can point our finger to, we lean.

We get to walking crooked. Typically unaware until we look up and see how unfamiliar things look. Or we run into a wall. Cattywampus creeps upon us while we're otherwise engaged.

On the rare occasion—when all the stars align—lateral movement can help us float like a sidewinder snake above the hottest desert sand and over the dunes with ease. But generally, it's a detour we could do without. In the best case, it throws a hitch in forward progress. In the worst, it can unravel all sorts of carefully stitched together seams. Regardless, no one is immune. Austyn was right, "Sideways does feel crazy, GG!"

And it happens all the time.

Stuck

In the check-out line at Target, I found myself mindlessly singing under my breath, "Baby shark doo doo da-do-da-do, baby shark doo doo da-do-da-do." I'm not sure I would have even realized what I was doing had I not noticed the woman in line in front of me bobbing her head along with the beat. What is it about children's songs that make them play inside your head like a phonograph needle stuck on vinyl? It's as if their melodies are coated in pine tar. You can't shake them if you try.

It's funny the things we get stuck in and the things that get stuck in us. We get stuck in traffic. We get stuck in jobs. We get stuck in the ruts of our daily lives. We get stuck on the phone, stuck on an idea, stuck on a bad date, stuck on a word. We high center, stranded with all wheels off the ground. And then unable to gain enough traction to grip and move on, we flounder. Like a fish on the bank, we flop around helplessly, knowing where we want or need to be, but having absolutely no idea how to get from where we are to there. *Stuck* happens on all kinds of levels and only occasionally is it fun.

Sometimes we can sense *stuck* coming. Like water in the bathtub as it gets sucked toward the drain, we can feel it ominously swooping in. Other times, it just comes out of left field and entombs us while we are minding our own business—being where we're supposed to be, doing what we're supposed to be doing. We look up one day and we're frozen. We're stuck in a body we don't like. Or a life we don't want. Or a quagmire we can't seem to wriggle free from.

Almost anything feels preferable to being where we are.

In whitewater rafting, the term for stuck is *wrapped*. A wrap happens if the inflatable raft hits a current broadside and gets slammed into a rock. The rushing water bends the raft around a rock where it gets wedged with the weight and movement of the current holding it in place. If you've ever ridden the rapids, you've probably found yourself in one. One minute you're whooping and hollering as you speed across the white-capped water, and the next you're not going anywhere. You're between a rock and a hard place, inconceivably and irretrievably stuck.

Within seconds, you almost lose your mind. Something about being unable to move makes your insides eat themselves.

Rafting experts have some simple suggestions for getting unstuck. And contrary to common supposition, rarely do these remedies involve assistance from those not in the boat. First, experts say, "Do not make matters worse." I can only guess this is placed as a preamble because most people usually do—first make matters worse, that is. Second, they say, "Assess the situation and stabilize the scene." In other words, define the circumstance without the pomp. Get exceptionally clear on the facts. Then, once an ordered stage is set, these are the things they suggest you do to get free.

Number one: Shift your weight.

Simply make a physical move. This seems to work (for scientific reasons I have neither the ability nor the desire to explain) for any sort of *stuckness*. The blank page is staring at you? Go to a different room. Sit in a different chair. The problem is at an impasse? Drive an alternate route. Talk about it on the patio. The movie in your head is playing on a loop? Run. Jump. Stretch. Do anything you can dream up to jiggle the crystals that balance your brain. Sometimes they'll slide right where they need to be to trigger the trap door that will open and set you free.

Number two: Lighten the load.

Figure out what you have with you that's not essential and get rid of it. Excommunicate the clutter that you thought you might use, thought you were supposed to bring, or just thought looked cool loading into the boat. Most of us typically carry way too much.

Without the excess baggage, sometimes the boat will simply release itself.

Number three: Bounce on the tube.

Dial up the kid who might be napping in your heart and play. Pretend you're a four-year-old at a bouncy house, cut the reins and jump. It won't take long to feel better, even if the boat doesn't budge. But bouncing has a way of leveling out pressure points. There's such freedom in letting go.

Number four: Find the friction and dismantle it.

Order matters. There's a reason experts suggest you do this last. It's not always easy to identify where the rub is, and it's sometimes brutally difficult to eliminate it once you do. But on occasion, the deep dive is necessary. When nothing else will liberate you, the points of adhesion have to be painstakingly addressed.

The good news is that if you're stuck, you're not alone. Millions of people are trapped in their own mire right beside you. And all of us, desperate for extrication, would like nothing more than for someone on the shore to toss us a line and pull us out. Unfortunately, that's not exactly how it works. Breaking loose may ultimately be a group project, but we each play the lead role in our own rescue. If we want to get unstuck, we have to free ourselves.

10

Unexplainable Tethers

How long is infinity? Start measuring; say good-bye to living. How do you explain the never-ending sequence of pi? Ask a math guru; prepare to lose your mind.

What came first, the chicken or the egg? Plead the fifth; or just take the rooster.

Questions without digestible answers make us crazy. We want to know! We ache for proof that will fit in our palm.

But some concepts are too big to contain.

Just because we can't wrap our arms around something doesn't make it any less real.

Grandparenthood

A guy standing in line at the airport Chick-fil-A had on a white T-shirt that simply said in black bold letters across the front, "**Jesus.**" If you ask me, the period made the shirt. We were on our way back from a fundraising event in North Carolina where a ten-year survivor of stage four metastatic breast cancer made us laugh, think and give. Hurricane Ida had just slammed New Orleans (on the anniversary, no less, of Katrina), and we were dodging her afterbirth through Atlanta as we hustled to get home. The terminal televisions displayed the devastation in Louisiana alongside the political upheaval overseas while people swirled like maggots avoiding contact and wearing masks.

"Jesus."

Like an interrogating attorney asking questions he already has the answers to, that T-shirt tied it all up in a bow. Five letters and a period. "Jesus." It sounds so simple when you put it like that.

In 2021, Colton and Morgan brought home a tiny wad of perfection balled up in the middle of a baby car seat we affectionately called the armored cradle. Both sets of grandparents and one very invested aunt had submitted projections on how much the baby darling would weigh when she arrived. The closest in proximation to the exact birth weight would win the prize of holding her first. I don't play slots, I don't bet on horses, and I rarely get the good hand when someone passes out the cards. But somehow, I got lucky on this one. Six pounds, thirteen ounces won me the coveted prize.

As I struggled to unstrap the newborn (a task I should have taken a class for), I couldn't help but think she looked like a caterpillar missing her cocoon. And that I had gotten lucky at precisely the right moment in time.

Some things are big, and some things are Julia-Roberts-Pretty-Woman Huge. But the day you hold your first grandchild for the first time doesn't fit on any scale. It's a cousin to double rainbows and sneaky sunrises that spill out of the sky like a tie-dye ribbon out of a magician's hat. Heaven-sent stuff. "How Great is our God" would not stop playing on a loop inside my head.

Everybody says grandkids are the best. "If I had known they'd be this good, I would have had them first." We heard that more times than we can count. It's funny and at least more than sort of true, as best I can tell. I have already discovered that the view is vastly different from the backseat of the car. Parents sit in the driver's seat. They have to. It's their job to get their kids where they need to be. And I'm not referring to soccer practice or dance lessons. Parents' eyes are supposed to be on the road. They don't have the luxury of studying auxiliary things.

Grandparents, however, get to gawk at the flowers in the median and monitor the roadside construction. It's more than okay if we read billboards and turn around to look at souped-up cars we pass on the road. We don't have to worry about changing lanes, going the speed limit, or navigating congested traffic. We just get to ride and soak up all we see.

Those first couple of weeks, Colton would carry Austyn around on his forearm like a football, her pallet the acreage between his wrist and elbow, his hand the headboard anchoring her in place. Those days went by fast. The weeks went faster. I'm still mad about the pictures we didn't get to take because she changed too fast for us to snap. Austyn's parents do the laborious stuff - the bottles, the diapers, the letting her cry herself to sleep. I do all that, too, except maybe the cry herself to sleep part. But I've also spent entire days staring at her while she breathes. That's a luxury only grandparents can afford.

Grandparenthood comes along right where it's supposed to in the continuum. I used to say that life felt backward. We work while our children are young, when we're constantly in chaos with too much on our plate to say grace over and never enough hours in the day to do it. Then we get older, our children leave home to begin lives of their own, we quit our jobs, and there's nobody to look after and nothing to do. I've always thought that was so upside down. But I get it now.

Grandparentland is a place you have to live your way to. No one would be any good at it if it had come first.

When I was younger, even if I'd had the time, I wouldn't have used it well. I would have been a backseat driver instead of a grateful companion riding along enjoying the view. I was too focused on building too many things—home, family, life, myself. I was the quintessential goal setter, the list maker, the driver with my hands at ten and two. I felt responsible for so much. Even for enjoying my kids. When they're *yours*, the ones that come squirting out of your body, you live a little worried that you will screw them up. So, a lot of what you do is laced with pointed purpose.

By the time you get to Grandparenthood, you realize you're not as powerful as you might have once thought. The pressure to do it right bled out of that balloon a long, long time ago. You recognize that right is relative, raising kids is something you do on a case-by-case basis, and that in the end there's a lot of luck involved with those who turn out well. In Grandparentland, time isn't tethered and doing it *right* never crosses your mind. You just hope you do it well, as you let love pull you wherever it is it wants you to go.

At not quite six months, our treasure has a tooth, an almost crawl, and a personality like her aunt's, the kind that never makes you wonder where you stand. She has a giggle (prompted mostly by her dog) that once you hear, you crave like chocolate when you're on a diet. It is invasive, addictive and it alters the way the blood moves through your veins.

I snuggle this wonder child often. I kiss her even more, and I have an entire scrapbook on my phone with pictures of her hands.

"Jesus."

I know no other way to fathom the pudgy fingers cupped around my shoulder as we rock or dance in the kitchen to her daddy's favorite country songs.

We walk underneath the canopy of trees a lot, this baby babbler and me, her chubby hand clutching the neck of my shirt, her round, blue eyes drinking in the dancing leaves as they're tickled by the wind, and I covet her awe. I want to can it in mason jars with screw top lids and give it away on the street corner like the rural farmers do their leftover tomatoes and their corn. If all the world could see as she does, we would live in a different sort of place. Babies cut the cataracts off your eyes.

God knew what he was doing when he made these little-bitty creatures. But he really hit a home run when he let our kids have kids.

A chunk of grandparent joy comes from watching your tow-headed toddler become someone's dad. Observing it is like going down a giant hill on a slip-and-slide. It's impossible to be anywhere else in your mind while it is happening and as soon as it's over, you want to do it again. When Austyn laughs, she looks like her daddy. When she gets excited, she looks like her mom. And when she's not at all about what's happening, her bottom lip flips down and she looks exactly like her daddy's sister's picture, the one that hangs outside my bedroom in the hall. The pieces of so much we love are decoupaged into this brand-new human who, in the end, is nobody but herself. Grandparent glasses allow us to see the pieces and the whole, the possibility without the probability, and the space that's needed in the middle for doing somersaults along the way.

Grandparenthood lets you relive all the highlights of your own parental journey, like a shuffling Rolodex of "Friends" episodes. The one where he went camping . . . the one when he got a dog . . . the one where he wore goggles and floaties . . . the one where he got stitches on his face—leaving you to marvel at how in the world that little curly-haired boy got to here. Here, where he makes bottles and changes diapers and knows all the words to the songs on "Go Dog. Go!" When Austyn falls asleep on her daddy's chest, I feel like I won the Super Bowl, but I'm not exhausted, and my lower back doesn't hurt.

"Jesus."

There's no explaining why hurricanes hit where and when they do. Or why the cancer warrior bucked the odds. Science says she shouldn't have, yet I hugged her twice this weekend. I can vouch for her. She's real. And I will never understand how a baby comes to be, regardless of all they teach us about it in school. Some things are too big for explanation.

"Jesus."

I gotta get me one of those shirts.

Unmitigated Favor

Peggy Noonan was President Ronald Reagan's speechwriter. In her book about him, *When Character was King*, she devotes a chapter to his humor. Finding the funny and creating it when there wasn't any was one of Reagan's gifts.

One display of the President's quick wit in action occurred

in 1981 when he and the First Lady hosted a state dinner for the president of Venezuela. At their request, Frank Sinatra, their dear and trusted friend, handled the entertainment. In addition to his performance, Sinatra decided to jazz things up by inviting Robert Goulet to join him as the main event. Sinatra planned to warm up the crowd and then turn them over to Goulet, the Broadway and Vegas headliner, in an attempt to loosen up what is a notoriously stiff event. Goulet, in that vein, did not disappoint. Most of his borderline and below-the-line songs (as well as the jokes he told in between) worked. Or at the least were tolerated. But he told one joke near the end that landed with a thud.

Goulet told a story about touring in Tahoe. He said the crowd there was a dud except for this one gorgeous girl in the back who he pitched all his songs to, flirting with her salaciously all night. It was only after the fact, he told the White House guests, that he discovered the beautiful woman in the back was the biggest transvestite in Tahoe. He said, "It all worked out, though. He writes me every week!"

Badum tsss.

The joke fell awkwardly into a sea of silence as the uncomfortable crowd shifted in their seats. Sideways glances cut everywhere as people, embarrassed, self-conscious and offended, were afraid to move their heads. Goulet sang one more song, Sinatra came out to close-up the entertainment, and shortly thereafter President Reagan came out to thank the crowd for having dinner at the White House. The President thanked Sinatra and then said, "And thank you, Bob Goulet, not only for entertaining us with your wonderful voice, but for remembering our night in Lake Tahoe."

The audience erupted.

All the awkwardness, the anxiety, the discomfort with what had been said went racing out of the too taut balloon that Reagan masterfully untied. He took a ticking time bomb and diffused it at the mic. The state dinner went on to be a beautiful, relaxed, laughter-filled evening that would be tagged by any standard as an unequivocal success.

If you put what the President did into a category, it would go into the bucket *Social Grace*.

Grace has many meanings and applications. We use it to describe a ballerina's twirl, a receiver's catch, or the way a confident person strides across a room. We use it to encapsulate goodwill and to express honor in attendance. In the Christian world, we use it to put a label on the thing that saves the day. A gift we receive from God that we do not deserve.

Yet grace is one of those things that's really hard to *get*. We know it when we see it transform hearts, soften blows, and mend dilapidated fences. But it's tough to say exactly what it looks like. Things with hard edges are difficult to define.

The gifted writer, Anne Lamott, says, "Grace meets us where we are and does not leave us there." Of all the explanations floating around, I think I like that one best. Her implication: Grace's work is bridging gaps.

We seem to find this invisible gift easier to understand when it's vertical. We *kind of* get it when it's coming from God. He's lofty, somewhat mysterious, and capable of things we on Earth are not. But even then, it seems above our comprehension line. The word *grace* floats around like the word *faith*—in the clouds where we can't touch. So, we struggle when we try to wrap our heads around how it works from side to side.

Perhaps on this earth, grace is akin to allowance. Not lack of accountability or a free ticket to ride on a gravy train, but room for all those things that we simply cannot know. Grace says, "I forgive you," when there is no apology spoken. Grace says, "I love you," when junk is in the way. Grace says, "I believe your best intention," regardless of the action that got twisted in release.

Basically, grace says, "You lunged for the edge of the pool, but you aren't quite there yet. These next six inches are on me." It says, "I got you." And then it gets you, as Lamott says, on down the road in "ever so slightly better shape."

Grace saves.

It changes the way a situation or a person or a moment looks and feels, because it's an inside job. It changes the looker, not what's being looked at. Grace bastes a soul like my Granny used to temporarily hinge a hem. It holds things together while gently carrying us where we need to go. Grace is kindly and relaxed . . . less judgy and conclusion-ish . . . more forgiving and inclined to leave the door slightly cracked. It washes whoever lets it with a reminder that everything has something worth saving, even if all the parts look wonky and the finish is rubbed off.

Grace covers everything. The gaps. The mess. The hurt. The confusion. The toe stubs. The gaffs. The overlooks. The underdones. It coats it all.

And the best part is, it always lies in waiting. All we have to do is let it in.

11

Perfect Imperfection

You have no idea what to do when somebody first lays a baby in your arms. Even if you've taken all the classes and devoured all the recommended books.

Nobody can tell you how to do it right because the target jumps around. Parenting is not a perfect process.

It's "more here," "less there," "don't do that again," "do this next time" followed by a staunch resolution to simply stay the course.

It's a recipe in flux.

Love – especially the familial kind—is inexact.

Mother Made

If you're reading this, you have one. Or you had one—though I can't imagine a mom being past tense even if she's gone. It's the universal tie that binds, the inextricable link of life. We are because she was.

And is.

And forever more shall be.

Mothers have the most demanding, integral job on the planet—and yet what's crazy is nobody knows how to do it. None of us. Not even the supermoms who self-profess by the stickers on their SUV's back glass. We all just grope around in the dark, hoping against all hope that we don't break things as we go. Yet, mothers are supposed to *know* . . . how to do things, when to do things, what the best things are to do. So, we try. But the dirty little secret is, we do a lot of guessing, too.

The truest confession I ever heard from a new mother about her hot-off-the-press child was, "I don't have any idea who she is, but she sure does." Maybe I love her sentiment so much because it sort of summed up my baby number two.

My second child, Chandler, came reluctantly (we thought) because she missed her arrival date by over a week, and I had to be induced. However, we quickly discovered we'd mis-tagged her tardiness. Not that she wasn't ready, but more so that she was warning us we better be. She came in on her own terms, serving notice. When they first laid her on my chest, she looked up at me with these giant ocean-blue eyes—not writhing, not crying, just looking—straight at me as if to say, "I'm out now and I've got my own ideas about how this thing is going to go."

When said child was somewhere between barely two and almost three, on a casual drive from Oklahoma City to Norman, she put another pin in the ground. From her snuggly-safe car apparatus in the back seat, we found ourselves at an impasse over some earth-shattering matter I can no longer recall. In short, I had a plan for her behavior, and she saw it a different way. After going back and forth over the top of the head rests, I laid down the gauntlet, "You say one more word and I'm going to pull this car over and spank your bottom!"

To which my precocious daughter replied, "Word." Defiance laced with sarcasm—at two!

Obviously, my child had given me no choice but to pull over and follow through on my threat. I could see it, somewhere deep in the unwritten handbook of Mothering for Dummies was a chapter on always doing what you said you were going to do. So, I did. As cars zoomed by at alarming rates of speed, with my vehicle parked but running, I jumped out slamming the front door as I lunged for the back so I could rush in and pounce. But before I could squeeze the handle, the baby culprit pushed the lock button and with a grin as big as Dallas began to victoriously clap her hands from the other side of the glass.

There I stood on the shoulder of the highway, my toddler locked-in and me locked-out, solidifying the fact that I was pretty much unfit to be anybody's mom.

Oh, the things children teach us, mostly about ourselves.

My firstborn was a pleaser. He did what I asked him to do. He was adventurous, fun, and happy in the way that Disney dreamers aim for when they sit down at their desks to create. Colton was high-energy and rambunctious, but he was easy. Easy in a way that juked me. It made me feel like I had somehow cornered the market, that I'd stumbled upon the mummying secret. Like maybe I'd figured this thing out.

But you've already met Chandler, so you know that wasn't true.

We have ideas, us baby-bearing creatures. We have things we envision ourselves teaching our kids and things we imagine them doing. "Look both ways before you cross the street." "Be kind to others." "Share your toys." "Say your prayers." We see them in Easter clothes and Halloween costumes. We see them leaving cookies and milk for Santa as well as hay and water for the reindeer he'll leave parked in the backyard snow. We see them in prom regalia, high school jerseys, caps and gowns, and wedding whites. But there is so much that isn't visible when we draw the future inside our heads.

It never works out exactly like we think it will. Mostly because we have no way of knowing who these teensy people are. Not really. Even when they grow inside us.

We think our job is to *make* them—to make them into something or someone. But our job is really to supply them room to make themselves.

Guiding a child to adulthood is daunting. We try to teach and model morals, values, friendship, boundaries (lived by and broken), self-expression, confidence, empathy, work ethic—all the things we know they'll need in the world outside our walls. But the internal and external wrangling involved in learning . . . that's for them.

Missing Abyss

I miss my dad on my birthday. Every January 19th I have a pang. It would sound way better if I said I miss my dad on *his* birthday, in February. I do. But not in the way I miss him on the day that marks each trip of mine around the sun.

I don't remember squat about my birthday observances when I

was a kid. I think we traditionally had a homemade cake with some candles on it, but I can't really say for sure. I might have even had a party or two, although birthday celebrations then were nothing like the full-scale Broadway productions they have now become. Mostly, a birthday party in the 70s had to do with chocolate cupcakes, polka-dotted napkins with tiny matching cups that could be purchased at Ben Franklin's for less than five and a dime, and a game of Pin the Tail on the Donkey taped to the aluminum siding of the carport wall.

As my brother and I got older, birthday gestures from our parents morphed from presents to cards. Mom's were a precious sentiment wrapped around a bit of cash. Dad's were stupid funnies with an extra-corny nugget added below the punch line in his signature LOVE, DAD. When we moved away from home, mom's cards kept coming, but somewhere along the way dad's birthday wishes morphed from a card to a call. A call that was more of a jukebox tune than a phone conversation. I'd say "Hello" the way we do with an uptick at the end, and seamlessly, as if someone had punched B53, my dad would launch directly into "Happy Birthday." A carefully curated version he had written specifically for me.

He sang it traditionally (not messing with the tune the way we often do with it and our country's anthem). He sang it slowly, never rushing while clearly pronouncing every word. He also sang it opera style—baritone or high soprano. Sometimes, if he was really feeling his oats, he'd alternate between the two with every other stanza. It was an impressive performance for one not classically trained in anything other than carry-a-tune. He sang it completely, bulling right through the hitchy part in the middle where most non-singer singers get self-conscious and wither away. Dad's enthusiasm never wavered as he crooned his way to a flourishing finish of differing octave "many mores."

On January 19th, I could not wait for the phone to ring.

To be clear, these serenades were silly. Sometimes hysterically so. But they were also thought out with keen rhymes that tied into something at least semi-relevant to either or both of our lives. When he finished singing, I would simply hear a "click."

When loved ones are no longer with us, we live with a pervasive void. Sometimes it fills up with rich re-runs, sometimes it's just a cavern full of empty ache. Missing comes in all sorts of shapes and textures, and none of them feel the same.

The kind of missing that bubbles up on my dad's birthday is the grown-up kind that's littered with funeral flashbacks and a poorly put together movie of his last six years of hard days. Fun stuff co-mingles with it, certainly—the legendary Saturday-morning breakfasts, pots and pans clanging well before any reasonable person (especially a teenager) would want to be awake . . . his golf swing . . . his fishing tackle . . . the meticulously organized barn where he ran his side-hustle painting signs. But most of all, on Dad's birthday, I grieve that he isn't here. I ache for all he doesn't get to see and do.

When I miss him on *my* birthday, I ache for me, not him.

I've spent a good bit of my life trying to be a grown-up, even before I was one. I am the self-designated *doer of hard things*. But in my big-girl life, on my birthday—for a second—my dad's singing phone call made me a kid again. It was permission to be silly while also acting as a bookmark. He was who he was, and that is who he would always be. Regardless of age, his or mine. My one and only dad.

Every year on my birthday, his absence hits me. Right between the eyes.

I'm not sure when or how it happened—whether my brother took the baton before dad passed or if he reached back to grab it the following year—but the birthday serenades continue. My brother is so much like our dad. Sometimes when I listen to the rhyme unfolding, between the giggles and my shaking head, I force myself to remember dad is not the one who's singing. The pang is as real as ever, but it doesn't last as long. And for a minute, just like always, I get to be a kid again.

The Accumulation of Time

Something happens to a man when a baby comes along. Something happens to everyone remotely connected to the baby when a baby comes along, but the shift that occurs in a dad is palpable. It's like his skin turns inside out. The tough stuff is still there, it's just way more concentrated in certain areas and way less all-inclusive. Suddenly, there are fissures where things can travel in and out.

Fatherhood affects a man's eyes, too. What he looks at changes within seconds, but so does how he sees things when he looks. It's as if they hand out 3-D glasses after delivery. When he sets his eyes on this tiny human who has his ears and *not* his nose, he can see the child in the present, then the future, and then forever in one fell swoop. That's a lot to process, especially when you feel responsible for all that lies ahead. Unfortunately, or fortunately, depending on how you look at it, the glasses never come off. They come with the goody basket, the baby blanket with the hospital logo stamped in the corner, and the sitz bath instructions for mom. They're dad's part of the gift package given to parents when they take their baby home.

Society tries to tell us that dads should be supermen, "Don the cape and save the day!" But super men do a whole lot more than protect, fix, and solve. Dads earn their title in the boring everydayness of being around. Not all their jobs are big, bold, and loud. Most of them aren't any of those things at all. The malleable little people for whom they are responsible need soft nudges, bumper guards with give, and enough room to find their way. Quiet things that rarely make a scene.

They also need models and directives, pokes and prods, discipline and accountability—all those hard to wrap your arms around things that can overwhelm the most diligent and prepared. I've often thought that might be one of the reasons some dads run—sheer terror at the thought of all they have to be and do. They never run for lack of love; you can't convince me *that* is even a thing. They just can't see themselves as having all the stuff it takes to wear the title well. I wish they all could know that no one has the stuff. Everybody builds it as they go.

I heard a story once about a woman who lived on an obscure piece of land hidden from public view by a grove of trees. To get to her place, you had to know it was there and be willing to go looking for it to find it. Those who did were always glad they made the trek.

What you'd find once you made your way down the graveled path that cut through the undergrowth of unkempt land, was a majestic hillside of daffodils in every color. Five acres of flowers planted in swaths of cerulean blue, butter yellow, tangerine orange, and vibrant fire-engine red. The side of the mountain looked as if someone had poured vats of colored paint from the top that froze into ribbons of grandeur on their way down. The sight was breathtaking for everyone who viewed it. Word got around fast—it was worth a see.

So, the owner of the property posted a rickety sign on the front porch of her modest cabin, the place that she called home. The sign simply read:

"Answers to the Questions I Know You're Asking"
1. 50,000 bulbs
2. One woman, two hands, very little brain
3. Since 1958

The story is, apparently, true. It was first told by Jaroldeen Edwards who coined the term, *The Daffodil Principle*, and wrote a book with the same name. Every year, for over forty years, in the San Bernardino Mountains, Gene Bauer planted daffodils. Edwards told Bauer's story, then wrote about it. For decades since, the story's been repeated around the world.

I think about it, and her, on Father's Day. I also think about my dad, my husband who is a dad, my son who is a dad, my friends who are dads, and the young men who I once taught who are now dads. I consider the dailiness of their charge—the showing up part that refracts continually—whether or not they are conscious of their actions. By how they walk, talk, laugh, think, play, work and pray, they leave pieces of themselves in those they shelter and clothe. Ordinary adds up.

It's the accumulation of time that does the molding. It makes both parties who they are.

I never once found a Father's Day card I thought fit my dad. What he'd end up with every year was something supposedly funny about golfing or fishing or farting or picking your nose. My dad wasn't a "come -sit-on-my-knee-so-I-can-teach-you-scripture" kind of dad, but every Sunday you could find him in his pew at church. He wasn't a lecturer or a sage advice-giver or a booming professional success in the way the world hands out its marks, but he taught me how to swing a club and a bat, how to plant a tree, edge a lawn, and draw letters flawlessly to scale. He loved me and my brother unabashedly and he did the father thing the best that he knew how. His try was perfectly imperfect—it gave us both room to become.

I hope dads get it. That the simple wonder of their love and presence has mystical powers that make up for all they don't know how to do. Sometimes in their urgency (egged on by the world) to be all things grand and emphatic to their children, they undervalue the shaping power of uncomplicated, bottomless love. It takes neither talent nor education to wrap a child up in agape. Days spent doing that will take care of all the rest.

12

Campaigns

It's easy to get obsessed with audacious goals, measurable skill sets, statistics, intricate processes and systems that determine quality while building exquisite efficiency.

It's also easy to miss the connective tissue that lives between such BIG IMPORTANT THINGS.

It all matters. But how we handle the human bits influences both the experience and the bottom line.

Laughing All the Way

The Savannah Bananas are a traveling baseball circus that, since 2016, has turned America's favorite pastime upside down. For twenty-five bucks, patrons attending Banana games receive a ticket for two hours of dancing, singing, acrobatics, plus all the food and drink they care to consume—and baseball. The Bananas' organization has one goal: make baseball fun. Their home games have a wait list 60,000 people long.

Jesse Cole, the puppeteer of this genius enterprise, set out to do things differently than the big leagues customarily do. In addition to superior fan engagement (including special rules like if a fan catches a foul ball it counts as an out), the Banana organization does things the baseball world—much less the *business* world—can't fathom. Things like securing zero sponsorship, phoning every fan who purchases a piece of merchandise, charging zero sales tax, and shipping items for free. The added values go on and on and on. Baseball is the show, but the sidebars and the free stuff are the magnets drawing people in. Laughter is, however, what keeps them coming back.

Want a tribe, a team, or a family to work? Give them something to laugh about together and they may never come undone. It's the "Ancient Chinese Secret" often undervalued and impossible to overuse. "The family that prays together stays together," so the saying goes. The one that laughs a lot does, too.

In 2023, after the Boston Celtics dug a 0-3 hole in the NBA semi- finals series vs. the Miami Heat, veteran Al Horford told his coach to ditch the film session and send the team to Topgolf for the day. Apparently, the Celtics spent the next 24 hours laughing at Horford's swing. (And at and with each other for a litany of things.) The team stormed back in game four—again in game five—then again in heroic fashion at the buzzer in game six before ultimately conceding to the Heat in the final win-or-go-home game. Without question, Horford's team excursion alleviated some pressure by zooming out for a bit beyond the bubble of their high-paying, high-platform job. But what it also did was what laughing does. It melded people together in places well-meaning words and intentional gestures don't have the ability to reach.

Sometimes all you need to do to come together is share a belly laugh.

Two decades earlier, our women's basketball team had a cast of characters who could all really play ball. We had players who could shoot . . . players who were good at getting fouled . . . players who could defend, players who could pass . . . players who could rebound even though they weren't very tall . . .. Off the court, they were equally diverse. Some were loud, some were quiet. Some were studious, some were silly. But when they got together, they had one main thing in common. What they loved to do more than anything (even play basketball) was laugh.

During a particularly daunting stretch of conference road trips, our staff made the executive decision to ditch the customary night-before-the game review of the scout. Instead of gathering to watch film of opposing players, we gathered to divide up into teams to play homemade games.

On the eve of a Big 12 match-up in Manhattan, Kansas that could clinch us the conference title, we played an epic game of *Concentration*, a popular TV game show from the 70s where contestants matched prizes represented by squares on a game board that revealed a picture puzzle underneath. That night, in the middle of nowhere in a janky Holiday Inn, the picture underneath the puzzle was a rapper known as Ludacris and a race car known for speed.

Kansas State was good. Really, really good. They had talent at every spot and all kinds of size that we did not. But we had one thing, maybe, they didn't. We were really fast. Hence the message: Ludicrous Speed.

I remember everything about that night before the game. I remember the cramped hotel "suite" we were all stuffed into like sardines. I can hear Roz and Caton arguing about who screamed the answer to the puzzle first. I can see Steph Luce jumping on the chair. I can feel my side stitching as my eyes leaked. I don't think I'll ever forget the way we all rolled around begging for breath while cackling like out of control hyenas as our players fought to win that silly game.

We laugh about it still.

We laughed about it in time-outs the next day during the forty-minute contest (which we won). We laughed about it on the bus on the way home. We laughed about it in San Antonio when we were waiting in the locker room the day before the Final Four. We laughed about it at our twenty-year reunion when we came back together to celebrate our run.

And every time we do, it's like an invisible pinky swear.

Laughter does a lot of fabulous things for our well-being. It strengthens our immune system, reduces our stress, stimulates our mental acuity, softens our jaw, and helps us look at ourselves and the world through a more colorful lens. It's also a beautiful conduit for connection. When we laugh together, we stick.

Don't Be Dumb

My number one best friend and I have a thing we say to each other when one or the other of us is behaving like a toddler. I might self-deceptively whine about what a bad friend I've been (the kind of whine that's really designed to elicit reassurance that I have not, in fact, been a bad friend at all). Instead of *that*, she gives me, "Don't be dumb."

Likewise, she might go on about how she's not sure if she can do a thing—how it might be beyond her ability—though there's never been a thing she could not do once she set her mind to it. "Don't be dumb" will be what I say as if it is a conjunction, moving us on to other things.

It's a pivoting phrase for us. A gentle tap on the shoulder which urges us to get over ourselves. And at its utterance, we do. We get on about the business of whatever is next. It's a tool we've used for years to keep us from carving out angst holes where a peaceful road should be. But its usefulness doesn't stop there. "Don't be dumb" also serves our friendship by jolting us to see the obvious when our eyes are glazed, or by reminding us, when our emotions are peaked, to simply walk away. That simple phrase tethers us to a way of behaving that helps us be who we most want to be. Individually and together. It's become our iron string.

That's something every heart is in need of, especially ones that are bound together. Ones who, on their own, might naturally vibrate to very different things.

Those responsible for the behavior of others are taxed, at the start, with creating a set of rules, standards, or expectations for the people in the group. Anyone who is in charge—CEOs, managers, coaches, parents—knows clear expectations are the linchpin for positive group results. "Culture" is the hot word we wrap around that concept these days, but that's really just a trendy way of saying "this is how we, as people in a group together, have agreed we will behave." As leaders, we get it all muddied up sometimes. We overthink and overstate, and though our manicured set of behavior guidelines comes from the best of intentions, our desire to be thorough drives us to be anything but simply clear. So many things matter—respect, love, trust, accountability, discipline—the list goes on for days. But a too-long list can get confusing. Words that don't convey action float in the mind like puffy clouds that are impossible to get your arms around. I know I was forever guilty of asking for too many invisible things.

If I had to do it again, I'd throw my dart at the heart of the matter and let the margins take care of themselves. I might pare it down to this. "Do Your Job, Pick Up Trash, and Don't Be Dumb." In the spirit of "less is more," I really think this about covers it.

Whatever the *it* might be.

What organization wouldn't be better if everybody in it did their job? Not what they call fun. Not what they deem to be important. Not what they imagine they'll get the biggest bang for doing, but the job they've been assigned. This is not to suggest we stay within prescriptive borders never going above or beyond or helping one another along the way. Work continually overlaps. But things that come apart at the seams typically start unraveling when someone doesn't do what they are supposed to do. They drop the ball for all kinds of different reasons—laziness, incompetence, distractedness, mental or physical fatigue, or wanting to get fired instead of quitting the job they don't want. When people don't take care of their responsibilities, bad things happen. If we could only remember to worry most about the things with which we have been personally charged, a lot would get done better. And faster. And a whole lot less would come undone.

I'd also hold a hard line when it comes to trash. This may seem like a picky detail, but it's an outgrowth of a bigger picture that has to do with where you keep your eyes. Before you can pick up trash, you have to see it. And you can't see it if you're always otherwise engaged. That means you can't walk around with your eyes on your phone, or your head stuck up your backside, focused only on your narcissistic self. People need to look up and out to see—to make things better in whatever way they can. Even if it seems minuscule at the moment. "Picking Up Trash" also means that you recognize your role as a steward of the planet and the people on it—a person who comes after one and before another—a cog in the chain link of civilization who bears the responsibility of taking care of someone and something other than yourself.

The rest, I think, gets covered in the vat of "Don't Be Dumb."

I have a preacher friend who says new Christians sometimes ask him how they are supposed to know what they should and shouldn't do. He said he just tells them to write "Jesus is the Boss of Me" on a sign and hang it by their bed.

That supplies about all the intel one might need.

Desired behavior never *just happens*. It's not a cosmic explosion, but more likely a boring march of sound decisions, often nudged by a verbal rudder fashioned out of everyday words.

Shake It Off

When Austyn falls, bumps into something, or drops a book about Peter Rabbit on her foot, her inclination is to cry. Usually, there is a pause—a space between when the hurt happens and when the hurt that happened reaches her brain. In that blink-and-you-miss-it gap, she's learned to make a decision about how she will respond.

What she does is "shake it off." Literally.

She shakes her hair, her skinny arms and even her legs, one foot at a time. It's her way of not getting caught up in the momentary hurt. It's her way of dancing with it and getting it out of her system. It's her way of moving on.

But moving on gets harder as we grow.

Humans are natural-born collectors. We hoard. Our cabinets are full of things we used to like or once had to have or might someday come to need. We have tools we cannot find, clothes we cannot wear, along with dishes we will never ever use. For a myriad of reasons we usually cannot name, we simply cannot bring ourselves to throw the stuff away. Even once we figure out that it no longer serves us, we keep it in the vault. We don't only do that in our houses. We also do it in our heads. Possessions aren't the only things that take up precious space.

Gathering and collecting actions, comments, and opinions has become the new great American pastime. We amass what fallible humans do and say, hoarding gestures, words and phrases as if they were fashioned with intent to pierce us to the bone. Some are. But many aren't. Often, the people behaving poorly or making statements we find painful are not thinking of us at all. We're not the central character in everybody's tale. And yet, we grasp at actions and utterances of others, clutching them to our chests as if they were pre-ordained to live inside our soul.

Moving on is not a thing we're very good at anymore.

Growing up, my friends and I were peppered by "Shake it off!" Maybe it's an old-school thing, or a small-town thing, or an Oklahoma thing, but somebody shouted it toward me at least once a week. That's how it was in the small southern town that raised me. As a softball player when I'd get nailed by an errant pitch, I'd hear "Shake it off!" as I tossed my bat and jogged down the first-base path. At the free throw line after an important miss, I'd hear, "Shake it off!" come at me from the sideline or the bleachers as the referee handed me the ball for a second try. When I tripped and fell or dropped the ball or scratched my knee or cracked my heart, someone was always not too far in the distance making sure that I moved on. "Shake it off" is among some of the best advice I ever received.

I have a sign hanging in my living room that displays the "Four Agreements." The author's code of conduct, devised to limit personal suffering and create a conduit for joy, is based on Toltec wisdom. Don Miguel Ruiz's agreements boil peaceful living down to a simple four-pronged charge:

"Always try your best. Be impeccable with your word. Don't make assumptions. Don't take things personally."

In my mind, when I read the first two, I hear someone yelling "Just do it!" When I read the second two, I hear "Shake it off!" How to successfully keep going can maybe be whittled down to that.

My granddaughter's ability to move on is not innate. Her parents taught her early that "shaking it off" is something she can do in lieu of crying if she's so inclined. And so, it has become a visceral reaction to her dents and dings. It's what she does to get past the pain to whatever fabulous wonders might be waiting around the bend. And wondrous stuff is everywhere. Life proves that to her every day. It's a deal, I feel quite certain, she is already glad she has made.

For some reason, we grown-ups have a harder time with letting go. We like to hang on to stuff that happens and stack it up in piles as if space were infinite—like we won't run out of room. But we will. And we do. Then we have no place to put the things we really need to keep. In addition, the hurts we save get heavy. Carrying them around makes us tired, out of sorts, and ultimately less nimble for avoiding future scrapes.

Hazards lie hidden. It's impossible to move through days and weeks (much less months and years) and not get scathed. The nicks are part of living. They're the price we pay for being imperfect humans striving for perfection in a less than perfect world. But we don't have to make every stumble an *ordeal*—some things we can just wriggle through and shake them off.

The Laundry List

I'm not much of a New Year's resolutions girl, but I do love lists. They erect borders around slippery things I'm afraid might slide away if I don't step in and do my part to contain them. The ones in the notes on my phone, while a decent substitute when I'm on the go, don't hold a candle to the real ones I make on the backs of envelopes—the ones that sometimes get re-written just so they can get checked off. Those carry gravitas in their etching.

That's how stuff gets done.

It's how the filter on the fridge gets fixed, the coat closet gets cleaned out, and the doctor's appointment gets made. It's how the dog gets fed, the oil gets changed, and the Bible gets read. My lists hold things that are really important, commingled with a bunch of stuff that really isn't. Not in the grand scheme of things, anyway. They're a hodgepodge of new thoughts and old reminders. A governor for days to be proud of when I lay my head on the pillow at night.

"How we spend our days is how we spend our lives," said the brilliant writer, Annie Dillard. Our days, if graphed, would show up in messy, uneven layers as opposed to linear lines. While the peaks and valleys that mark our journey might not appear on the backs of random envelopes, the laundry list that does provides the girth. The story of our lives live there.

I once heard a tale about Michael Jordan—well after he had become MICHAEL JORDAN—playing in a pickup game back in North Carolina with some of the Tarheel players in the summer. The story goes that he angrily kicked a ball up into the rafters after his squad lost, prompting a guy on his team to mutter under his breath, "Geez. It's a pickup game. It's not *that* important."

Jordan's retort, as legend has it, was, "Important? Nah, it wasn't important. But it mattered. (Insert a few choice words). Everything matters."

The items on our laundry list are rarely *important*. They're things we want to do or need to do, with "have to do" hardly ever factoring in. But they matter. They matter because typically they are things that make all the other things we do possible. They are the proverbial extrapolation of putting rocks in a jar. But they also matter because they make up our days.

A laundry list is a life plan with its sleeves rolled up. It has a tedious core.

Most things of significance do.

Jane Kenyan and the poet Donald Hall were married for twenty-three years. She was forty-seven when she died. He said: "If anyone had asked us, 'Which year was the best, of your lives together?' we could have agreed on an answer: 'The one we remember least.' There were sorrowful years—the death of her father, my cancers, her depressions—and there were also years of adventure: a trip to China and Japan, two trips to India; years when my children were married; years when the grandchildren were born . . . . The best moment of our lives was one quiet, repeated day of work in our house. Not everyone understands."

And even those who do, don't usually realize it. Mundanity isn't shiny, so it's super easy to miss.

The laundry list gets us from Monday to Tuesday and January to December and down the road toward twenty-three years. Sometimes it houses the regimen of big dreams, sometimes the formation of new habits. But mostly, it's just an intentional way of using the hours God gives us in a day.

We learn, over time, that the dull, sometimes tiresome activities of life are not merely items to check off once they are completed (though it feels quite good to do that). The matter matters, too.

13

Footprints

Footprints are made to be stepped in. Unlike fingerprints, which are intricate one-of-a-kinds, footprints have a shape but no definition. One size fits many.

Strung together, they create a trail that acts as a suggestion for when we are lost, unsure, or just beginning to map a course.

Tracks left by others give us an idea of where and how to go, but they leave wiggle room. Space to be us inside them.

Conviction

My dad's dad was a reader. The house he shared with Grandma on Plato Road had a library right off the front living room that was stuffed like a sausage with books and collections of periodicals. The occasional table beside his chair in the living room always housed three things: a pungent pipe, a scratched-up magnifying glass, and at least one or two well-worn editions of *National Geographic* magazine. Back editions of the clearly identifiable, yellow-rimmed covers formed a tower in the corner of the library floor. I never knew if Grandpa Buben saved them all or only his favorites, but they drew me like a magnet, mostly for the pictures, of course. That's the way *National Geographic* told the stories of the world.

Since 1888 *National Geographic* has been the photo album of our values, our lifestyles and our relationships with ourselves and one another. A close look at historical documentation shows a chronology of shifting norms and customs, an evolution of people, ideas and the societies that grow from those collisions. It displays our triumphs, tragedies, gaffes and our change-the-world moments in time. It's all there in vivid focus and glowing color for anybody who wants to look. Like the untouched skin of an elderly woman's face, the legend of our life is there.

I once heard Susan Goldberg, Editor-in-Chief of *National Geographic*—the first and only female to hold that position—deliver an acceptance speech for an award she was given in recognition of her trailblazing career. When she opened her mouth to speak about the iconic magazine, the floodgates of my memory opened. I could smell my grandpa's pipe and see my brother's ginormous fish eye through the back side of the magnifying glass. I felt the brazen resignation of the Nigerian woman with steely eyes, a ring in her nose, and golden earrings as big as her head gracing the cover of the magazine. I had never seen anything like her. Thumbing through that publication stretched the boundaries of my world.

Photographs can tell a story sometimes in ways words can't. In her speech at the Annie Oakley Awards, Goldberg said a lot of important, impressive and funny things about her journalistic path and her life inside the belly of this historic publication. But what stuck with me was a photo from a series on "Women in the Military" that she projected on the screen. The picture hangs on the wall in her office.

It's a photograph of USMC Corporal Gabrielle Green carrying a 200-plus-pound fellow Marine across her shoulders as she runs up a ramp. You can't be a Marine if you can't do this. Everybody, regardless of gender, understands why. But the juxtaposition of the woman and the man both wearing Nikes and military greens is arresting. The physical arrangement is not the one we expect. When we look at it, it's as if the ghosts of the road less traveled seep from the pixels to our eyes. We see Corporal Green's tattooed quadricep billboard *"The fire inside me burns brighter than the fire around me,"* and though we mostly can't relate to the power it exudes, we feel the words there in the chambers of our soul.

Who among us hasn't had to summon *that* to get from some unsustainable here to a scary but far-away there?

Ms. Goldberg said she loved the look in the corporal's eyes and the words inked on her thigh. She said the photo synthesizes resilience for her. And that she finds all the picture shows, plus everything it represents, empowering. She also said it serves as a literal reminder of our responsibility to lift one another as we go.

Amen. It made me think about all of that, too.

And it also made me think about Mary Lou Retton. I was a freshman in college when she looked straight into the camera before vaulting into the all-around gold medal at the 1984 Olympics. Her vault was historic. A perfect ten. Beautiful and emphatic because of the moment and the stage, but also because of the extraordinary skill a lifetime of commitment to a craft put on display. I don't remember anything about the vault, except that she stuck it. The look in her eye before she did, however, is burned into the gray matter of my brain. She not only knew she could, she knew she was about to. Her conviction lassoed every heart that watched her do that thing she loved to do.

. . . and I thought about a picture I moved from my office at the gym to the office at my house when I retired from collegiate coaching. The snapshot is of Stacey Dales at center court in the Alamodome in San Antonio immediately following our victory in the National Championship semi-final game. The picture caught Stace's essence. It still calls me to move toward it, much the way her intensity seduced me the first time I saw her play. Her steely eyes ooze capital *B* belief —the kind you tie your wagon to—which is exactly how we ended up at the Final Four anyway. When I think of Stacey, I always think of her exactly in that way.

Conviction. The unapologetic kind that builds roads where there are none. The kind that makes the world a better place.

I know nothing about Corporal Green, but I suspect she wanted to be a Marine for a long time before she became one, probably more than she wanted anything in the world. The no-look look on her face says she is precisely where she wants to be, doing things she's absolutely sure she can do. Carrying this guy to the top of the ramp was not the culmination of anything. It's just one of a myriad of things she does because she is a Marine. That is who she is, who she was in her heart all along even before she passed the tests. Even before they put the stripes on her cuff. When I look at the photo of her, I see a woman in the middle of the muscle convicted about her ability to do whatever is required of her.

The look in her eyes is eerily similar to the one I remember so vividly of the Nigerian woman on the cover of *National Geographic* in 1975. Different decades. Different countries. Different cultures. Different opportunities, different fences. Similar conviction.

The eyes of determined women look the same.

Teach a Man to Fish

With about ten minutes to go in the third quarter of the Thunder-Pelicans game, Jalen Williams drove the left lane line, picked up his dribble due to traffic, and found three Pelican defenders staring at the ball. A prescient Josh Giddy ran a back cut from the corner which Williams instinctively rewarded with an old-school bounce pass that Giddy kissed off the glass for two.

And I immediately thought of Robert Montgomery Knight.

In my first year as a head basketball coach, I taught my high schoolers to run Motion Offense. Continuity offenses, the ones living at the other end of the spectrum, never appealed much to me, perhaps because my jumpy mind went haywire during the predictable patterns that were easy to learn and a yawner to practice. The Flex Offense was especially vogue at the time, but its back-and-forth and back-and-forth again reflexive action (hence its name) made me want to poke my eyeballs out. True Motion, however, spoke directly to my heart. "Poetry! This is athletic poetry!" I thought when I watched it, long before I understood what it actually was or how it worked.

Then I began to study it and fell head-over-heels in love.

If you want to learn how to do something, you look long and hard at whomever is currently doing whatever it is really well. The man who taught "poetry in motion" better than anybody on the planet was an intolerant giant who had a gift for saying things in a way that made you not forget. He could be found in Bloomington, Indiana wearing a red sweater and a scowl, but he shared his "gospel" freely in clinics across the land. I attended every one I could get to. I ordered his videos. I bought his manuals. I immersed myself in the art of motion offense, then transferred all I learned to the players on my teams. Teaching it was, is, and probably always will be my favorite thing on Earth to do.

But nobody could teach the game James Naismith invented quite like Coach Bob Knight. For him, everything made sense—the when, the why, the what, the how. He could take the game apart and put it back together as if it were a puzzle made for children under ten.

The first time I saw Motion Offense played, the dimension of it captivated me. Then once I learned what the guts looked like, I was hooked. The endless possibilities that grew with each twitch of every player on the floor kept the lid off perfection. You could keep getting better and better and better no matter how good you got because the extrapolations were only limited by the imagination of those reading and reacting in real time on the court. The rhythm, the delicate balance of screening and cutting, the spacing and timing the offense was predicated on were fun (but hard) to teach and rewarding (but sometimes frustrating) to learn. Once you understood it though, the game switched to ultra high definition. You could see things in vivid detail you previously never even knew were there.

They say the great ones do that—they see things others don't. Prescience is certainly a trait we could ascribe to Bobby Knight. But his gift was greater than what he saw. Where he excelled was in getting others to see it, too. Nowhere was that as evident as in how he taught his players to play on the offensive end.

Coach Knight believed what you did when you *didn't* have the ball in your hand was just as important, if not more so, than what you did with it when you had it. Purposeful movement was his sermon, selflessness plus trust were the scripture and the verses, discipline was the invitation song. Once teams were baptized in the system, they ran on autopilot. They didn't need set plays to score. In the church of the General from West Point, advantages were created by players who understood how to play the game.

The first trip our Oklahoma Women's Basketball team took to the NCAA tournament was in the spring of 2000. The March Madness bracket sent us to West Lafayette, Indiana for the first two rounds where after winning game one, we found ourselves in a tussle in game two as we faced the Purdue Boilermakers, the defending National Champions, on their home floor. We trailed the entire game, but somehow kept hanging around.

In the final minutes, we found ourselves down one point with possession of the ball, so I called time-out and drew up a play, Our team left the huddle, took the floor, and ran it to perfection.

Too bad it didn't work.

On the heels of the failed attempt, however, our All-American point guard did what she knew how to do. Stacey Dales took the ball to the center of the floor so it could see both sides. What it saw when it got there was Laneisha Caufield, Stacey's back-court teammate, being closely denied beyond the three-point line high on the right wing. Stace took one hard dribble at Neish who took two steps toward the ball before planting her foot and cutting directly toward the rim. Stace led her with a bounce pass that she corralled and laid off the glass while simultaneously being smacked by two desperate defenders. The ball rimmed out, but whistles blew and Caufield went to the line. There she promptly sank two freethrows, giving us our first lead of the game.

When the final buzzer sounded less than a minute later, we were headed to the Sweet 16.

Lots of coaches reached out in the weeks and months following that game as ESPN had whipped around to the final minutes from all their various coverages across the map. Coaches wanted to get our "play." Unfortunately, I had to tell them we didn't have one. My guys made the play all by themselves.

They hadn't needed me to hand them a fish; they knew how to catch one. That win belongs, in part, to Bobby Knight.

I had coach's aphorisms all over my office and his teaching points appeared regularly as the "Thought for the Day" on our practice plan. On my credenza lived a Post-it announcing, "It's not what you teach but what you emphasize." We had, "Teams don't get beat on help, they get beat on recovery" on a sign in our locker room lounge. And we talked regularly, as if on a contract, about fostering the will to prepare, as much as the will to win.

I am not alone.

Bob Knight's teachings are embedded in coaches everywhere, regardless of the innovative offenses they may run or the defensive wrinkles they've added to their systems over the years. When meticulous practices are being planned or every toe is behind the line, a hint of Coach is there—and will continue to be there long after those in the trenches have forgotten from whom or where it came. And when the Mavericks zip the ball around like a hot potato, or the Celtics set a screen and second cut, or a high school squad from Lomego, Oklahoma runs the "give and go," a portion of the credit goes to the stubborn genius who taught us how to play.

The Kindness Club

The best thing about being a major college basketball coach for a quarter of a century is the people the platform allows you to meet. Because I was the coach at Oklahoma, I had the opportunity to meet billionaires, world-renowned musicians, Hollywood movie stars, and Oprah (yup, *she* gets a category all her own). I've met incredibly intelligent people, side-stitch-funny people, eccentric, interesting people, and crazy artistic people, but I've never met anybody more impressive than the children and the families who I met at 1200 Children's Avenue in Oklahoma City, the place where little people go to get well.

Through the years, my team and I had the privilege of hanging out with Batman, Superman and queens in various stages of their regalia. We had races down the hallways and puppet shows in the lobby. We played monumental games of Duck, Duck, Goose. We painted finger-and toenails, played video games, and shared our favorite songs. We named stuffed animals and played Hide and Seek with little green army men, while painting lots and lots of pictures, and making lots and lots of crafts.

And every time my team and I walked out of Children's Hospital, we bounced out better people than we were when we strolled in.

Giving is tricky-slick like that. It can make a U-turn in mid-air. Newton's Third Law says for every action, there is an equal and opposite reaction. Well . . . not really. Not at a Children's Hospital, anyway. There, when you empty the contents of a thimble, a five-gallon bucket comes back in return. We'd walk from the hospital to our cars every time with hearts so full we could barely shut the doors. Those tiny giants on the tenth floor doled out perspective like Walmart greeters do hellos. Unconditional love slopped all over every single thing they touched. It dripped from us on our drives back down the interstate toward home.

We learned a lot, my team and me, from the miniature superheroes at Children's Hospital. Things like patience, courage, honesty and strength. They taught us about kindness, gratitude, resilience, faith, the power of prayer, and a level of peace that can only be found when we turn absolutely everything over to God. We learned a lot of things from a lot of different kids at a lot of different times throughout the years, but the one pervasive sort of non-negotiable that showed up without fail was how to be purely present wherever you are. Those kids sit in it. However ugly the *it* might be. And they wring the minutes dry. They don't wallow. I've never met one who felt sorry for himself or whined about "why me?" Not one. And they fight—Lord, do they fight—with the kind of grit bound by sinew that we all wish our teams could have. These children are always exactly where they are. Planted. Present. Not scattered, as most of us visitors tend to be. It's like these little angels scored a fast pass to wisdom with their admission bracelet to the tenth floor, a coupon that allows them to simply let it be.

We can learn a lot when we let ourselves be present. Even in— and perhaps especially in—the truly tough places where it's scary and painful and impossible to understand.

It's a truth commonly acknowledged by those in the problem-solving business that the people who have the problem usually know the most about what they need to solve it. Context matters. People living in the muck have context in spades. Kids with cancer are no exception. They can't cure their own illnesses, but they often have some answers to some even bigger stuff. Bigger than childhood cancer? We can't even imagine. But children frequently wear x-ray glasses that cut through all the crap. The heart of the matter tends to be where they most often strike.

Like my friend Keaton, for example. He was seven years old when he founded *The K Club*, five years after they found his leukemia. Going to the hospital was all this little man knew. So, in turn, he found going there quite grand. At Children's, he ruthlessly charmed the nurses and entertained his peers while encouraging his parents and making the rounds to see all the patients who were new. At the Jimmy Everest Cancer Center at Children's Hospital, Keaton Barron was a spreader of joy.

In January 2018, on the heels of five years of chemotherapy, radiation, T-cell therapy, medication, and doctors' orders that made ant trails across his days, Keaton was admitted to the hospital for the flu. That's when *The K Club* was born.

The K Club was the brainchild of Keaton and God's special agent, Kay Tangner, who spends her days loving kids who are fighting for their lives. Together, she and Keaton carefully laid out all the rules. The membership fee would be one dollar, or "whatever a person can afford," and the money would go to charity. Keaton designed and drew an official logo, named Strawberry Cereal Bars as the *K Club* snack, appointed therapy dogs as the *K Club* mascot, and designated the hospital chapel as the Clubhouse home. Together, the team of Keaton and Kay made membership cards to be used as kindness batons, complete with his trademark striped "K" on the front and the club's Bible verse on the back. "Just so, let your light shine . . ." Matthew 5:16.

The original goal of The K Club was 1,000 members. As it turns out, though, that bar was kind of low. Within five months, the club paid for a fresh water well in the Democratic Republic of the

Congo and bought part of a cow through Heifer International. They also provided balloons and gift cards for families and patients in the children's ICU. The Kindness Club had members from all fifty states and several countries to boot. Keaton chaired the mission from his hospital bed for a while. And then from his bed at home before he went to meet his maker on May 11, 2018.

His star shot quickly across the Oklahoma sky, but it left an indelible trail.

In 2018, *The K Club* became an official corporation and then a full-fledged non-profit raising over $100,000 annually. Keaton's parents, Luke and Holly, live his mission. *The K Club* is their kindness car, the vehicle that enables them to impact families who are sitting where *they* sat. Keaton knew, as do they, what sick kids need and what sick kids' families have to have. So, there are Legos—lots and lots of Legos. And there are *K Club* hats and T-shirts because teams have to have team gear. There are balloons, care packages, scholarship funds for the ones who make it, and funeral funds for the ones who don't.

This is just some of the stuff you can see. The stuff you can't is impossible to list. Kindness, courage, compassion, and caring, those are the words of *The K Club's* mission statement. That's the pixie dust that keeps on falling from Keaton's trail across the sky. He had no clue about how to hide from cancer or out-run it or how to keep it from doing whatever it is it wants to do. But it appears he knew a thing or two about the world. And he was here long enough to know that kindness can be the answer to all sorts of messed up things. So, he created a system that would help him spread the word long after he was gone.

I keep a stack of *K Club* cards wrapped by a rubber band inside my purse. It's my random-acts reminder to be kinder than I might be inclined. And to pass it on, just as Keaton intended when he burst across the sky. For those who are interested in helping kids go to www.kclubkindness.org.

14
Transitions

The guy in line in front of me at the grocery store was wearing a Titleist golf cap. I asked him, "What's your handicap?"

He nervously laughed and said, "I can only *barely* shoot par on maybe four out of eighteen holes."

"I have an arbitrary question for you," I said. "You game?" Curious, he nodded, "Sure."

"Before you hit the ball off the tee, what's the most important quality within yourself you pay attention to?"

Immediately proud, he said, "Hips."

"I mean quality, not physiology," I clarified.

Swinging his eyes from the florescent lights back to mine, he reluctantly answered, "Calm." With an extra deep breath, "Calm. I need calm."

"How often do you get it?"

"Rarely," he replied.

Intrigued, I dug a bit deeper. "When you *do* get it, how long does it take you to find it? A few seconds . . . minutes?"

"When I go to the driving range . . . ahhhhhh . . . it can take forty-five minutes," he begrudgingly admitted.

"Thank you for playing," I said, as he grabbed his ice cream and headed for the door.

Shifting takes time

Coin Flip

In the middle of life, dichotomy reigns. "This stage is awful, and it's awesome," a friend so aptly stated as he weaved his way through an ordinary day that was suddenly anything but. "The highs are high, and the lows are low," he matter-of-factly lamented. In almost everything he touched, he could feel both sides of the coin.

Living does that after a while. It carves capacity within us. An ability to cup a good/bad thing in our–hands—gently, without flinching—while loving it and hating it in equal parts. These are "the best and worst of times" the classic writer described. A carousel age of love and loss and what rides shotgun alongside both. Days you wouldn't trade a thing for, yet days you'd give about anything to have taken off your hands.

The space between the two is thinner than a sliver of the moon.

Our earliest days, it seems, are spent chasing what we want. We soar and we get sucker punched. We scratch and claw and dig. But for the most part—though we fly and fall—the experiences of youth happen between the ends we cannot and do not touch. In time, we stretch. The days stack.

We build the things we imagine, the life we crave, or at the least a life we are proud to have, only to discover that everything comes with a timer. In a snap, we find ourselves hopscotching between the edges of paradise and purgatory. We love resolutely; ache in deep recesses we didn't know existed. Like a pinball, we bounce from gratitude to grief, and back again, knowing at once the excruciating heat and wonder that bubbles under either side.

And it catches us unaware. This foray into the mid-life land. We don't put on our blinker, carefully change lanes, and take the exit ramp on purpose. We just look up one day and realize that we're there, in this place where the tough and the tremendous are in cahoots together. Everything we love and live for is interleaved by difficult things.

I asked my friend who recently lost his father, "What is the hardest part?"

"Knowing what to do next," he said. "The grief drowns you, ya' know . . .," his words trailing off. "But then God . . . you know, he sends you these stones to step on . . .." His voice mirrored his forward motion while dragging a heavy heart.

We talked about the gaping hole that no one, despite their best intentions, will be able to fill. We talked about mortality and how quickly it can morph from a pedestrian word to an ogre who stands in front of you, boring a hole in your head. We talked about the time he and his father shared in his last days, how they simultaneously scraped his soul and yet are his most treasured prize.

You don't get one without the other, we both surmised. Love creates the crater. The crater holds the love.

That Age

"It was so nice to meet you," my friend's grandma said, as she watched him put on his coat to leave.

"It was nice to meet you, too," he said in return, as though their acquaintance commenced today. "I love you so much!"

His headline gift was shining. Chief among his collection of skills was his ability to meet people wherever they were. It was

Thanksgiving and the family had gathered after skipping the year before. The holiday itself felt strangely familiar, like an old high school classmate he hadn't seen in twenty years. Awkward, but recognized and appreciated, like it hadn't been in a very long time.

Feeling oddly buoyant as he left the facility and walked toward his car, my friend mouthed to no one in particular, "Thank you." He *was* grateful. Appreciative and aware—in ways perhaps he'd never been before—of the blessings that come from time spent with loved ones, even when loved ones can't remember who you are.

I'm at that age. The one where my contemporaries and I are watching our folks grow old and disappear. The conversations we used to have about what our children are into and what schools they might want to attend have shifted to taking the car keys away and paying for their care. It's brutal talk. The kind that makes age spots show up on your arms and Golden Goose tennis shoes seem sillier than they already are.

We talk about it all, my friends and me. In raw terms with exasperating detail. The dad who's gotten heavy, the mom who's gotten frail, the dad who sticks his spoon in his ear, the mom who thinks her son is her brother, the grandma who can't remember if her daughter's mom is alive. We talk about it because we have to, because we need to, and because we want someone to help us figure out what to do. And sometimes because it seems like fiction until the words make sounds in the air.

While getting older sure has its advantages, getting old is a whole other deal. And watching it happen to the people who raised you is the G-force of mid-life.

They say that as we grow older, our dominant traits keep growing, too. Like if your nose is large, it gets larger. Or if your ear lobes have mass when you're young, there's a chance they could graze your shoulders before it's all said and done. I don't know

142

whether it's true or not, but I feel like it is as I watch it play out with people I've known and loved.

The same often goes for non-physical traits. The thing that makes you distinctly you sometimes becomes what you most wholly are as you move toward the end of your life. For example, my dad was funny. Though dementia thieved his speech and his memory, it left his humor alone. His funny stuck with him—pretty much 24-7—down the homestretch. What a gift. Laughter—his and ours—became the pillows that cushioned the ride when the wheels on the wagon finally fell off. We list that as one of our greatest blessings when we count them out at night.

Unfortunately, the exacerbation of identifiable traits is not always good, especially if the dominant personality trait is less than stellar. Like a grumpy dad or a resentful mom. What was sufferable in moderation can be devastating in excess. I ache for my friends who have to navigate a booby-trapped path like that.

In some situations, it's just the opposite. Sometimes the elderly parent becomes someone he never was at all. That's how aging goes. The laid-back dad becomes the angry dad. The perky mom becomes the languid mom. I have a friend who never once heard her mother utter a curse word and now, she dog cusses every human (or ghost) in sight. It's cruel the way disease and time, or the combination of both, can take a brain as hostage and twist it however it wants.

It's hard to lose loved ones, no matter how they go. The last mile of the way is tough . . . and typically twisty, with blind curve after blind curve after blind curve. The roads all have uphill in common, yet each is as unique as the family through which it bends.

Process of Elimination

I figured out what I didn't want to do with my life in the summer of 1982. In between my junior and senior years of high school, I worked in a downtown office for an oil company about twenty miles away from the town where I lived. I dressed professionally every morning, made the commute, then sat in an office for four hundred hours a day, logging numbers for something that had to do with drilling. Mostly what I did was sigh a lot and pray for five o'clock.

I was seventeen and head over heels in love with basketball. And though I thought I wanted to coach and teach, the world felt so wide open. I could choose whatever path I wanted. So, I dipped my toe in corporate life, quickly discovering fluorescent lights, the same four walls, and filing weren't for me. The confinement made my skin crawl. I needed NOT to sit at a desk all day. Or deal with numbers. (I need words.) And I needed work that had blank pages instead of columns and a bunch of skinny lines. I wasn't convinced of what my future would hold, but I knew without question what it wouldn't.

Knowing what we don't want is sometimes just as valuable as knowing what we do.

The process of elimination is a strategy that works pretty much anywhere it gets applied. It's a help-along when deciding where to go to dinner: "I definitely don't want to drive all the way across town." "Seafood sounds awful right now." "I'm not in the mood to talk over a lot of noise . . .."

It's a game-changer when deciding what to wear: "That skirt goes with open-toe shoes. I need a pedicure, so the skirt is out." "No white pants—it rained last night." "I'm too fat right now to tuck in a shirt."

It works when trying to separate the chaff from the grain while dating, too, and it can play a pivotal role in helping figure out how to spend the days of our one-and-only lives. The process of elimination has transformative application to both the little and the big.

Many of my friends and peers are making professional transitions right now. They're leaving the safety and security of careers that have spanned decades for the new lane of "don't-know-yet." And as they prepare to make this jump, they think a lot about what they *can* do. As in, "what am I capable of?" *Can* matters, but a better compass is probably, "What do you really *want* to do?" I ask them because their lives, like mine, often are more than halfway over, but also because we're usually pretty good at the things we enjoy.

For people who have done the same thing for a very long time, deciding to switch horses or change streams can be precarious. "I've only been a banker, I'm not sure I know how to do anything else." "I've always been a coach. I don't know what else I can do." The list of transferable skills emanating from both (and most all others if we're being candid) is lengthy and everywhere applicable. But time can sometimes coax us into looking through a straw.

There's this 1990s movie called *At First Sight* in which Val Kilmer stars as a blind man who undergoes a breakthrough surgery to restore retinal activity. When they first take the patches off his eyes after surgery, everything is overwhelming. Life is big and bright, so he instinctively squeezes his eyes shut because it hurts to see. What he sees doesn't even really qualify as images, but even if it did, he wouldn't know the names to associate with it. He saw only chaos that made no sense to him. The doctor suggests he find one thing—it doesn't matter what it is—to look at *hard*. The attention will bring the fuzzy into focus.

Clarity starts with a place to start.

15

Rudders

The vertical axis that steers a ship through water does its work under the surface. It counteracts forces, minimizes mass and keeps a vessel on track.

If you'd never seen the underbelly of a boat, you'd have no idea.

Rudders work behind-the-scenes, like a stage manager in a theatre production, to ensure the course is kept.

The things that imprint us deeply—people, places, events and exchanges—become our invisible life-guides. By gently nudging, they help us stay in line.

Handed-Downs

I have a recipe drawer in my kitchen, though I don't open it very often. In it are six or eight cookbooks—several small-town, plastic-spined, put-togethers (fundraiser projects from the "county extension" way back in the day), one hardback from Ree Drummond, *The Pioneer Woman*, another titled *Desserts* I believe we received as a wedding gift, and one professionally published paperback from the Women's Auxiliary at Oklahoma Christian College that I wrote the foreword for. The greater contents of the drawer are handwritten loose-leaf recipes separated into categorical bundles secured by sturdy metal clips.

These are the things handed down.

The cuisine instructions from my mother-in-law are easy to spot. They're on matching cards with a black and white cow in the upper right-hand corner. Her beautifully legible prescriptions are detailed in ink in such a way that anyone anywhere could read and follow. There are directions for French pastry puffs, lemon squares, broccoli salad, marinade for kabobs . . . as well as a bunch of other dishes that call for ingredients it might take me hours to find at the store. Other directions, for things like chow chow and wilted lettuce salad, are on fragments torn from an address book in my Grandma Buben's German scrawl. One for homemade bread and another for beans and chili sauce are printed in my dad's professional ALL CAPS lettering on perfectly folded paper pulled from a legal pad. But most of the recipes in the drawer belonged to Granny.

They aren't mine that she made for me, they're hers that she fed us by. Hers, scarred with such loving overuse that they bring her back for a second when I hold them in my hand.

Granny's tried-and-trues are scratched on whatever happened to be within arm's reach at the time. Some are on the backs of envelopes. Others are sprawled across lined index cards. Some she scribbled on pieces of paper pulled from an Eck Drug notebook. All are smeared and soiled, and most have a dog-eared corner or an edge that's slightly torn. These guides to a domestic practice I never picked up are worth a fortune to me.

My drawer of chaos has a heartbeat. A personality. A "watch-this" spunk that you can't get from a cut-and-pasted link or a set of instructions floating on the cloud. Those random recipes, stiff from aged splatter and the oily fingerprints of busy hands doing too many things at once, reflect the people who wrote them down. They left the souls of themselves on the page.

After Granny passed, people I never met—some with last names I recognized, others with ones I didn't—sent recipes. Some of them were in Granny's penmanship, paper-clipped to a note explaining their familial significance of the particular dish she had once shared with them—a dish so delicious they asked her for the recipe once the food was gone so they could make it for themselves. Some were in someone else's loved-one's handwriting, family favorites titled: "Bill Claxton's Fruitcake" or "Bill's Peanut Brittle." ("Bill" was what everyone called my mother's mother before Granny became her name.) Making food was how she said, "I'm sorry," "Congratulations," "Get well soon," "I want to get to know you better."

Handwritten recipes were Granny's love language. Her culinary investment in others boomeranged back to me.

One package that came in the mail shortly after Granny passed included a note that read:

"I hope this reaches you personally. I've kept this recipe for years, thinking I'd mail it to you . . . I grew up in Healdton, Oklahoma, on Magnolia, about one block from your Claxton grandparents' store.

I remember Shorty and Bill with such fondness. It's sad that the small-town, love-your-neighbor attitude seems a thing of the past. It was such a wonderful childhood. This recipe was a favorite of my mom's (it's in her handwriting) and now in MY seventy-first year it dawned on me that if I intended to pass it on, I'd better get with the program . . .."

Unfortunately, handwritten cooking instructions are pretty much a habit of the past. We don't write much of anything with a pen on a piece of paper anymore. There are easier, more efficient ways to keep track of things.

Easier, but not necessarily better.

The recipe this woman included, transcribed in her mother's penmanship in 1964, is how good gets passed around. Clearly, it wasn't just about the cake.

Caked Into the Walls

I found the house that became our home on a walk. The ranch-style brick looked like an orphaned hacienda beyond the band of blackjack oaks that separated it from the street. Through the mysterious curtain of branches and leaves, a siren song wafted. The friend I was walking with said off-handedly, "That place is empty. Nobody has lived there for quite some time."

"Whoa. Wait up." I said, pulled by the lure of the camouflaged mess. "We should go look in the windows."

Ever enamored by hidden potential, my heart raced at the thought of what could be. A quarter-brick wall bearing an entrance but not a gate, surrounded an unkempt courtyard that sanctioned off the house from the yard. The double front doors were tucked inside it, flanked by floor-to-ceiling plate-glass windows, some partially clouded over because of broken seals. I cupped my eyes against a clear one and saw through to the backyard. The bones of the house took my breath away.

It was everything I'd dreamed of though not been able to draw or describe—a place with room to expand and contort, the sort of place where a life could fit.

Thirty-five years later, it is a part of me.

Dane and I bought the house on the street named for what it looks like in the fall, despite the chipped Spanish tile in the entry, the orange linoleum kitchen and the squirrels who had claimed the fireplace as their own. At the snail's pace that two high school teachers' salaries allowed, we tackled projects one by one, painstakingly transforming the neglected structure into a place where we could comfortably live. From there, it grew with us. It swelled to hold our babies and morphed to fit the vacillations of my taste. We would rehab it section by section, then we would ripen and rehab it over again.

Our home, like the family who loves it, remains a work in progress most of the time.

I appreciate new houses. Walls without cracks, doors that don't stick, floors that don't make things with four legs tilt. Although I do have great affection for an outlet where I need it, I can't imagine not having something begging to be fixed. An old house needs a keeper. I crave a reason to tinker. This place is the real-life Thelma to my real-life Louise. It knows me.

Most days (despite the currently-leaking shower), I can't imagine not getting to live here. From my see-through living room to the spots of exposed brick, to the bank of windows added to the kitchen during renovation number three, our house is a reflection of me becoming me, and us becoming us. It's unpredictable and imperfect—lacking in seamless flooring, cluttered by family photos, and without a box to check if you tried to define its style. But it holds all of me. The parts I shudder at, as well as the pieces that make me quietly proud are caked into the walls. The story of my life is here.

In the center of our home is a bank of cabinets and drawers—the only piece of the entire place that hasn't been amended. The dated woodwork represents an open loop I'm not eager to close. Like the Navajo weavers' tradition of a loomed-in spirit line, the needy sea of storage is a flaw left with purpose. A means of keeping a door ajar.

The places we call home don't necessarily include the address where we lay our head. Home can be a hiking trail, a church pew, or another human being, regardless of geographical coordinates. But a house that crosses the invisible line morphing into a home is a double bonus. It's both where you get to go and where you get to be.

A Great Place to Be From

As I drove past the pecan trees on the north edge of town, the substance of a place that never tried to be anything other than what it was washed over me. When I arrived to speak at Healdton's annual Chamber of Commerce event, it felt like I was surrounded by the community who raised me, though most of the people who did were long gone. That's the thing about a place people pour their lives into—it's as if they live on in the water. For generations, you can feel them in the streets.

Growing up in a small town gives gifts you can't buy on Amazon and have delivered to your door, though sometimes it's hard to see that while you're there. My Granny used to say, "So-and-so is standing knee deep in the river and dying of thirst." Unfortunately, that's often where you find yourself while living in a one-stoplight town. But then you leave and realize there won't ever be enough days or ways to say, "Thank you" for the reservoir you took with you when you went.

I won't be able to say it as cleverly or as succinctly as country songwriters do, but I'd like to give it a shot.

This is my attempt.

Dear Healdton,

Thank you, first of all, for staying out of the way. I know that doesn't sound like a compliment coming right out of the chute, but it most certainly is, even if it feels backward. Dreams don't grow well when hovered around. You gave mine air, access to the light, the room they needed to breathe. My aspirations had the space to work and root their way in, though you were not their partner in crime. You didn't clear any paths. You didn't write any plans. You sure didn't hold up a bar and say, "Touch this if you can." You just kinda said, "Get after it, Sally, if that's what you really want to do." And then you went on about your business and let me find my way. What a gift to have the freedom to grow not inside a jar.

The things we work toward because we want to, will always be the ladders we climb best on. I learned that from you.

Thank you, too, for the footprints. They were everywhere—in sizes large and small, in places I expected to find them, and in places I never dreamed I would. The "how-to- be" road map was always on display. You taught me that mamas look after children even if they aren't their own . . . that buying somebody's lunch without them

152

knowing it is a way to make a person's day . . . that you should purchase necessities locally, even if it costs a little more . . . and that if you owe somebody a nickel, you find a way to get it back to them, even if that means you have to chase them down. You lived out the long game long before "the long game" was something everybody thought was cool. Thank you for letting me experience the power of a village and feel the ripple effect of generosity. And for showing me that the extra effort required to make a thing right is always worth the work.

From you, I learned that a collection of people being all in, in all things, makes you different. It's like getting a ten-yard head start toward wherever you're trying to go.

Thank you for teaching me to show up. You taught me that it's important to go to school carnivals and buy ugly cakes that probably don't taste any better than they look. And to go to ballgames and root for the home team even if they aren't very good. You taught me to put on my boots and walk to church in the snow if the roads were too dangerous to drive on. And to find a way to go to weddings and funerals because beginnings and endings are precarious times.

Thank you for compelling me to do things I didn't want to do and learn things I never thought I'd need to know. The intestinal fortitude has come in handy, as has the confidence. Demonstrated ability is, of course, the birthplace of self-esteem. You gave me no choice but to build it by requiring I do hard things.

And, finally, thank you for your expectations. They weren't ever specific, but they were typically all-inclusive: everybody should do everything in the very best way they can. I felt that from every corner. It rose from the ground. Some might call that a heavy burden— a cross to bear and drag. But I never saw it as anything other than a blessing. It basically meant a whole bunch of people cared.

You never bulged with access to fancy things, but you tossed out opportunity like free candy from a homecoming queen in a parade. Everything we really needed was always within reach.

For these and all the little big things that give a kid a shot at the sky, I am eternally grateful. I can't think of a place I'd rather be from.

Once a Bulldog, always a Bulldog,

Sherri Buben Coale

About the Cover

I love the cover of this book so much—for reasons far beyond its depth and textures. It's an outgrowth of how one person leads to another who leads to another causing concentric circles to form. Confluence always astounds. The beautiful binding designed by Dana Bree, grew from the magical original painting of DeeDee Daniel, who was inspired by Yvonne, our mutual friend's wife, to paint. Yvonne acted, sang, danced and painted. DeeDee wrote music and took photographs. When Yvonne passed, DeeDee announced that she wanted to paint like "Y." And so, with her dear friend's art supplies, she began.

DeeDee has a studio in Los Angeles. I don't know her, yet, but I want to.

For more of the artist's work: artworkarchive.com/profile/blue-derby-fine-art

Acknowledgments

"We are like dwarfs on the shoulders of giants, so that we can see more than they, and things at a greater distance, not by virtue of any sharpness of sight on our part, or any physical distinction, but because we are carried high and raised up by their giant size."
—Bernard De Chartres

None of us get anywhere by ourselves. I am grateful to so many for being the gutter bumpers of my writing life. A smattering is mentioned here . . .

To my beautiful friend, with more book awards than I have shelves, who told me that most days when she looks at her work, she vacillates between "this is pretty good, and this is a total pile of buffalo turds." Thank you for reminding me that writing is hard. And that shipping it off for other people to read is even harder. And that we're never really sure about so much.

To the champions of my blog who tell me at church or via email or when we cross paths at a Thunder game, "That story hit the spot." Thank you for saying so. It always feels like confetti falling from the rafters when you do.

To my tribe of coaches that continues to expand even though

the sideline is no longer where I live. Strivers are bound by invisible strings. Thank you for scratching and clawing naked on the stage for all the world to see. Your courage changes things.

To Zach for counting my "ands" and (I couldn't resist) posting the numerical grand total in teacher-red ink before the title of every piece. Thank you for—with uber kindness always—nudging my punctuation. "Period inside the quotation marks, please." Thank you for waffling with me concerning shades of words, pushing me to tilt my head a different way, and routinely calling my bluff. You make me better by how you talk to me. "It is not often that someone comes along who is a true friend and a good writer," E.B. White said of Charlotte. Well, I suppose I lassoed the wind.

To my Gingerbread Friends—I couldn't possibly name you all, but as I've said before, you know who you are. Thank you for playing catch with me with an imaginary ball when my brain is blank. You make the good stuff even better and the bad stuff half as bad. Thank you for rooting for me (sometimes out loud but mostly under your breath) and for almost never rolling your eyes. I love you more than words.

And to my family—those who left a trail and those who are still dropping breadcrumbs from their pockets as they go. I live indebted. Mom, Bob, Jack . . . thank you for, you know, all the things the world never sees. Dane, Chandler, Colton, Morgan, Austyn, and Scottie (who just got here), thank you for the joy you wrap our days in and for letting me write stories about you that you and I both know are mostly true.

Finally, a special breath of gratitude to Austyn, for loaning me your lens.

Photo Credit—Shevaun Williams

About the Author
Sherri Coale

I love being called Coach. Still.

It's one of those labels . . . like Mom, or Sis, or GG (my newest and most favorite tag) that stands for more than what I do. It's part of who I am. My shoulders go back a little every time I hear it.

Coaching ball is what I did. For over 30 years. But it wasn't ever all I imagined doing.

So, in the spring of 2021, I retired from the dream job I had held at the University of Oklahoma, took my laptop to the backyard, danced around the table and started to write.

My first book *Rooted to Rise*, an Amazon excellent seller, was released in the fall of 2022. *The Compost File* is my third. The second, *Life Through the Eyes of a Point Guard*, continues to be a work in progress gently annoying me.

My husband and I live in the home where we raised our two children. I speak. I consult. I deadhead flowers. I smack tennis balls, jog daily whether I want to or not, and change my granddaughter's diapers.

I eat Jalapeno Cheetos every chance I get.

www.ingramcontent.com/pod-product-compliance
Lightning Source LLC
Chambersburg PA
CBHW051425090426
42737CB00014B/2838